The Newfound Legacy

IbbiLane Press

copyright ©2016

All rights reserved. No part of this book may be reproduced or utilized in any form or by any means, electronic or mechanical, including photocopying, recording, or by any information storage and retrieval systems, without permission in writing from the publisher.

Cover photography by Linda K. Webb, Woodinville, WA

Cover design by Leah Frieday

ISBN-13: 978-0692749142 (IbbiLane Press)

ISBN-10: 0692749144

"Rare is a young adult who has the discernment and understanding of how much their early childhood has shaped their lives. Add the usual childhood challenges the early death of a parent and child sexual abuse by a relative and you have a volatile mix of trauma, grief, a rollercoaster of emotions, and growing pains. This story by an amazing 17-year old is a testament to her emotional and spiritual maturity, self-discovery, forgiveness and healing. What a gift she gives to others like her to embrace their courage and open up about subjects that even adults find it difficult to face and discuss. Bravo to all of those who will be encouraged and healed by her raw, vulnerable and poignant story of transmuting pain into passion and purpose." Jody Rentner Doty

"A bright and talented young author, Alana retells dramatic stories of her life in powerful poems and memoirs. Alana is a gifted writer who has chosen to share her most personal narratives recounting the abuse she experienced as a child- something she has only recently recalled. I am proud to know this young woman who is such a positive role model and leader in her young years. She is making positive changes and wants you to be a part of that change. This book is meant to bring hope to many other abused adolescents, it's okay to speak up and talk about your experiences, it marks the beginning of the healing process and creates a healthy new chapter in your life. " -Jenniffer Eckert

"My dearest beautiful, first born Daughter,

From the time toy were conceived, you have always been in my heart and soul. Also papa's. With awe and love you have graced our lives from the day you were born. From your wide eyed first breath, you calmly turned your head in Papa's direction when he said "Happy Birthday beautiful Alana," you knew your name. It has been an exquisite ride watching you into the incredibly talented, loving, caring and wise beyond your years young lady that you are today. I know that your journey in life has not been easy, with darker times that you had to endure. As your mother I had to hide a lot of the terrible grief that I experienced when my instinct knew that someone else had harmed you, which we reported, but never knew who because part of you shut down the unfathomable abuse until the time when your mind allowed it to come out.

I never want you to experience how I feel regarding this issue. I am so very proud of you sweetheart. So grateful that you, as Alana, have decided to speak of it. To set the memories from your own soul with the dignity and grace of a warrior. I am so very glad that the process of writing your story has helped you. That you want to help others in their own grief and haunting memories. Break free of their experiences. To educate parents and teens/kids and give them strength to use their own voice. You can change the world, one word at a time. Bless you my love for being you. For inspiring me and others in so many ways. Shine on with your bright light and unending compassion. I will be here, loving you every day."-XO Mommy.

Publisher's Note

    This book is beautifully flawed and was intentionally left as written. It should be noted there is no table of contents as the author felt including one would "give away" her story and she wanted her journey to unfold for the readers in much the same way it unfolded for herself. Without a table of contents, page numbers seemed terribly unnecessary.

    I'm very proud of this young author. Her courage in coming forward to share her story will hopefully make it a little easier for others to come forward and share their own. Only by shedding light on the darkness can we ever hope to heal.

    ~Kellie Fitzgerald

Some names and details in this story have been changed to protect identities. However, it is entirely true. It is my story.

-A.L. Gorski Author *The Newfound Legacy*

"As a leader criticism is something you should expect"-Gleeson 2014

"To be beautiful means to be yourself. You don't need to be accepted by others. You need to accept yourself." -Bindi Irwin

Letter to the Younger Me 2005-2007

Looking back on the time period of 2005- 2007 I realize that those years were full dramatic amounts of change. If I could give my younger self advice knowing the challenges that I would face and the triumphs I would experience it would go something like this...

    Dear younger me,

    These next few years will fly by. There will be some challenging times and times when you will rejoice. Your new home of Washington has changed your life in ways that you have yet to fully grasp; with age knowledge of how dramatically it has changed your life will come. You will change schools one more time in 2006 to an amazing school in a small town about thirty minutes from where you currently live. You will also move to a new house on a small island that you will fall in love with everything about and get your very first job. Papa will also move to California right after you go back to Michigan for Thanksgiving. In California he will be living with his sister who you don't know very well but in the few times you have met her were weary of her. You were cautious for good reason, while you are there visiting do not trust her, she is up to no good. When you are at home with mommy and daddy in Washington it's okay to tell them if she did anything wrong to you even if she tells you not to. While you are in Washington with mommy and daddy you will make lots of new friends and be able to play with them as often as possible.

    When you go to California be cautious of your aunt, she isn't very friendly. If she touches you inappropriately it's okay to tell a trusted adult like papa, even if he doesn't believe you. When you get home tell mommy and daddy right away because they aren't allowed to ask. If something doesn't seem right, it probably isn't. The names that your aunt, uncle and one of your older cousins are calling you aren't what you really are. You are not a brat, worthless, a little shit or a tattletale. You are a beautiful blessing from God who has a place in this world; one day you will inspire many others by telling the stories of what is going on at the moment. Find the rays of sunshine and enjoy them when you can. Those evil people didn't take away who you are, they tried their hardest, but they didn't. Don't be afraid to stand up for what you know is right and wrong. Smile when you can and do your best to protect your little cousin and sister. They may think that you are the weaker of the group of you because you are a wall flower. That is far from the truth, you are observant and thoughtful. You watch every move they make. You try to do your best at everything which is what makes you amazing. Despite how things may seem at the moment, you won't have to see them much after the summer of 2007.

      Washington is your safe haven, as it should be. While you are in Washington be a kid because no one will try to hurt you or your sister. You are safe. You will also begin your first deployment with daddy for the military and find out that you are moving again after he returns home. A deployment is where moms and dads who are in the military go away for a while to other places to work to protect our country. When they leave its sad at first. However, you can still write each other letters and talk on the phone. This time daddy will be going to Asia for one year. He will bring home tons of fun things like Korean money and super soft pajamas. You will also experience your first ice storm since moving west. School will be out for two entire weeks! Grandma Mary will also move in with the family. She will bring lots of fun things with her including her cat Zorba who you call Zorbie. He is crazy and drinks out of the toilet like Princess (the dog) if you let him, he also loves catnip like Sweet Pea (our cat). Keep your head up. -Older you

Drunken Rages vs Innocent Faces

Note: This is a reflective first-hand account about an instance that happened in the spring of 2007. It is written as if it was in the now from the perspective of an eight-year-old. All names that I have not been given permission to use have been changed. Also the dialogue used is not exact as I was so young when it happened. Although I remember the day as if it was yesterday what people were saying is all jumbled up in my memories. Also "Uncle Butthead" and Uncle Ben are the same person. We called him "Uncle Butthead" when we thought he was being an idiot. We will call this rather tumultuous and frightful first-hand account Drunken Rages vs. Innocent Faces...

Dear Journal. Today was an okay day. Aunt Brie said some hateful things as usual, but she's gone for the night. I think she went out with some friends. So Tiffany, me, Marissa, Willow and Sydney are spending a hopefully fun night with papa and Uncle Ben. Papa is his usual goofy self, but Uncle Ben is acting weird. When he's around papa he's normal, then when he's around us only it seems almost like he's sleep walking.

Oh well, papa said that he has a quick errand to run. So we are staying here with Uncle Ben. On the way out the door papa told Uncle Ben to keep away from the booze. Uncle Ben told him that he would and promised him that he wasn't drunk. What is "booze"? Does booze mean alcohol? Yes, I have seen Uncle Ben drink way more alcohol sometimes then he should and get drunk. Is the reason that he's acting like he is sleepwalking is because he is drunk? Then he must be way more drunk then I have ever seen him. I have only seen him happy when he's drunk. So this could be scary. Should I be scared? Let me go ask Tiffany... She said maybe.

Oh no! I guess the answer is yes! I should be really, really, really scared. He's going absolutely nuts! Now is not the time to panic. I need to keep Marissa, Willow and Sydney safe because Tiffany doesn't seem to have noticed how nuts he's going. That and she's doing nothing about it! What the heck? What do I do? Should I call the police? Oh no oh no oh no!!! He's starting to tell us to "go fuck ourselves". What does "go fuck yourself" even mean? I know fuck is a naughty word, but what does it mean? Why is he acting like a monster?

Ahhhh!!! He's throwing things at us and Tiffany is packing a bag! She said that she has had enough and is leaving after she calls the cops. Wait, the police? Okay, that's a start. Phew! Finally, an end to this madness. Maybe not... As Tiffany dialed 911. Uncle Butthead threw a book which Tiffany jumped out of the way of that ended up hitting baby Sydney. Is she okay? The answer is yes. I think... She cried for a few seconds, but stopped. Thank God!

Uh oh... I didn't think she was actually serious about leaving. Wait Tiffany don't go!! Please stay!! She just left and locked the door behind her from the inside. Now is not the time to panic. As she was literally running out the door she handed me the phone and the 911 person asked me my name and papa's phone number. I told them. Then they asked me where I could try to go and hide from him. He's going nuts and Willow is on my leg shaking.

Okay, well here is a bedroom. I don't think I can go in it because Willow won't and I will not leave her alone. Hold on one second. I have an idea. I am going to ask Marissa to go in there and drag Sydney's bouncy seat in there with her. Then lock the door and hide the key. But where? Do it first, think second. Okay Willow lets have Marissa and Sydney play hide and seek. Marissa go in here please and sit on the bed so you can play hide and seek from Uncle Butthead. Sydney is going to be in here with you and play too.

Heck yes, they are both safe! Oh no, what about the key?! Um okay, I guess I will just have to put it down my pants. Ahhhhhh!!!! He's going to get us! Well not yet because Willow just kicked and punched him in the nuts. Hard!! Nice one Willow! Now I have to do something, quick. Because Marissa and Sydney are safe, but me and Willow aren't. What to do? What to do? What to do? Think fast, come on! We may not have much time before he gets up again!

There's an idea! The shoe bin! It's not very big and it's pretty full, but if we stand in it in a corner. We can use the lid as a shield and not get hit. Uh oh! He's up and starting to throw things!! At least we have a shield and chances are he's too drunk to think to think about lifting this bin up. Well, the police are almost here. I think, I hope! We may have to do something if they don't hurry!

He's coming at us again! He looks like a monster! Oh no, we have to do something!!!! Okay Willow it's time to play a game called fend off the monster. Willow: "Okay, how do you play? I'm scared!" It's okay Willow. I will keep you safe I promise. To play you throw things at someone scary like Uncle Butthead. Here is a brush next to the bin and it's pretty hard. Here Willow throw this! Good throw! It hit him hard and knocked him on his butt. Thank God!

The police are super close, only a few more minutes. Hang in there Willow, Marissa and Sydney! Only a few more minutes! We will be safe soon. I know it's been scary, but it will be over soon. Willow: "Why did Tiffany leave? Does she hate us?" I don't know Willow but we will be safe soon. Okay, I just realized that we have to somehow get to the door to let the police in. Excuse my language, but oh shit! He's coming at us! Again!!

Shoes!! That's it! We are standing in shoes. We can throw them at him and knock him over! It's time to do something. No time to think just do. Okay Willow, when I say go. It's time to play fend off the monster so we can let the policeman in to help us. One, two, three GO! Throw shoes at Uncle Butthead! It took a few minutes, but he's on the ground. For now, at least. After such a hard shoe (what I now know was a Stiletto) to the nuts I would be too. Not that I have nuts, but whatever. You get the point.

The police are finally here! All we have to do to get to the door is put the shield behind us in case he gets up. Okay Willow, it's time to get out of the bin and stand in front of me so we can get to the door. Willow: "Uncle Butthead will get us!" No he won't I promise; I will protect you. You get to open the door for the nice policeman who is here to help us! Willow: "Let's do it!" So next we ran to the door as fast as we could with our shield and I gave them the key to get Marissa and Sydney out of the room.

Right after that papa came back. Hugging him felt amazing. His arms have never felt so amazing to be held in. I can't even be scared anymore because of how happy I feel. The policeman told me that they were proud of me. I told them that I was just doing my best to do my job and keep everyone safe. I feel so loved but confused as to why we have to go to a hotel.

Oh well, sounds like it will be fun. We just got to our room and I am so tired. I feel so happy and safe right now. Mommy wasn't happy to hear about this. At all.

Love-Alana Gorski Age: 8

Looking back that day was utterly terrifying. Even writing about it is incredibly difficult, yet equally freeing. Despite how terrifying that day was, I learned my true strength from it. I learned to love deeper and to always go with my gut instinct. Had I not we all could have easily been killed. Our abuser who was my uncle and the father of Tiffany, Willow and Sydney, was over six feet tall and more than 200 pounds.

In the moment it failed to register with me the gravity of Tiffany's choice to leave. Recalling that day though, I forgive her. I feel a strong sense of anger, disappointment and disapproval of that choice simply because of how young I was. Neither of us was really old enough or equipped to deal with a situation such as that. However, had she stayed we probably could have all gotten to safety instead of only two of us being truly safe. In a situation such as that there is no way to get through to the abuser. Alcohol is an evil drug that alters the state of mind greatly which makes it even more dangerous and unpredictable.

That day was seemingly normal and my dad just went to run an errand not thinking that he was lying about being drunk. He like his wife was a master manipulator and was able to convince my dad of something that wasn't true. It wasn't for his lack of intelligence because once they get to that level of alcoholism it becomes easier to hide. Being held by our dad that day is something that I will never ever forget. On that tragic day I made a memory that little did I know would last a lifetime with that hug. There is always a positive in every negative situation. Since he is no longer with us here on earth I treasure that moment and often think of it during the times that I miss him the most. I thank God or whoever you believe in that I am here today because we all could have been killed. Lesson of the day: Abuse is terrifying and don't get drunk, ever. The potential consequences aren't worth a few hours or a night of fun.

Tattletale

To my abuser...

You may have forgotten the days that you violated me, but I never will.

Some may not believe me when I tell them what you did because my scars are not visible.

You violated me in a way that no one should ever experience, and threatened me with physical harm should I tell anyone.

At the time I knew what you were doing was wrong, however I did not know what to call it or want to get hurt if I did tell someone.

You thought that you had full control and in some demented way you did at the time.

Since that day my life has never been the same.

Not only did you do it once, you did it repeatedly. No matter how many times you did it.

I was still unable to understand what it was despite knowing it was wrong.

You took advantage of my age and innocence because you saw it as a weakness.

You repeatedly called me a "tattletale" during the times you were violating me and others.

You didn't kidnap me but due to circumstance, I stayed at your house for periods of time while I was visiting my dad.

This made you see me as an easier, weaker target.

Despite that I appeared weaker.

The truth is that I put up walls to appear that way and was finding my internal strength to force myself to get through the tough times.

It's not that it didn't hurt I just didn't show it in fear that there would be retaliation.

Each day that I went to bed I prayed that the next day would be free of your twisted abuse.

However, there was never a guarantee.

I tried to enjoy the days when you chose not to violate me in that way.

On those days I could try to claim the part of my childhood that you hadn't yet stolen into your devilish grips.

The days that you chose to violate me, the walls went up again making me feel worthless because I knew that I couldn't stop your actions while they were happening or take any immediate action.

On those days I felt as if I was an adult trapped in the body of a kid who was forced to grow up twenty years in a single day.

You also thought that what you did would forever go unnoticed. I am here to tell you that it won't.

It took me over ten years to understand what sexual abuse is and realize that it happened to me.

I am still coming to grips with what you did and will always wonder why you did it.

Maybe being a "tattletale" isn't a bad thing after all.

For almost a decade I allowed myself to believe that it was.

That is no longer true.

On those days you took away part of my innocence and instilled fears in me that are seemingly absurd to other people.

Those fears and the memories of those times will never go away.

Sometimes I have to put up the walls that I did while you were violating me just to get through the day.

It is on those days that I try to draw strength knowing that I have a purpose on this world.

You may not have thought or still don't think that I do.

That's okay with me because for so long I felt that I needed validation for every action that I took.

Most likely that in some way was because I tried to make sense of what you did to me.

Truth is there is no reason for the inexcusable actions that you chose to make.

Hence I no longer search for validation.

You taught me to never try to make sense of anything that doesn't immediately have a reason that it has happened.

It may have taken years to realize that and allow myself to fully understand why trying to make sense of certain things is pointless.

I have now accepted the truth and allowed myself to try to grow from that.

Being a "tattletale" as you so called me isn't such a bad thing after all.

If standing up for what I know is right and wrong makes me a "tattletale" then I am proud to be one.

Being willing to be a tattletale has allowed me to grow.

This tattletale is going somewhere in life despite all of your best efforts to stop me.

I will never ever forget what you did to me, but I will move on.

You didn't break me, but you tried. I hope that you know that.

Yours Truly

Signed

The Tattletale

The Demon They Call Cancer

The Demon they call cancer hits all too close to home.

It claimed the lives of not one but two of those I love all in nine months.

It comes quickly and unexpectedly, with no discrimination of gender, age or race.

The demon they call cancer comes in many forms, some more rare than others.
It transforms those who it affects in more ways than one.
They whittle down to only skin and bones or quickly gain weight from the medications they are given. Some even lose their hair.

The demon they call cancer kills some of its victims, while others and their families live with its effects of it for the rest of their lives.
Some of its survivor's bounce back to their new normal within a few weeks or months.
Others struggle to put their lives back together for many years.

The demon they call cancer tries to tear families apart.
Yet it usually strengthens those bonds it tries to break.
Despite what they go through many of its victims have resilient spirits that grow stronger as things get harder.

The demon they call cancer made me who I am today.
It taught me to not take a moment for granted.
Although I miss those closest to me whose lives it claimed, I know they wouldn't want me to dwell upon it.

The demon they call cancer will one day be nonexistent.
Until then some will tragically lose their lives and others will defeat it.

Yes, it is a tragedy, but we must focus on the positive and work towards a brighter future free of the demon that they call cancer.

In Loving Memory of my dad

James Anthony Gorski

March 5, 1966 - November 24, 2008

Letter to the Younger Me 2007-2009

Dear younger me,

The abuse is now over however these next few years will be some of the most challenging yet. Papa will be diagnosed with cancer in November of 2007, which you will find out about around Christmas time. Although the past few years with papa have been rough, you will learn the true meaning of forgiveness. You will learn that no one is perfect and papa will admit to his wrongdoings. These next few years will be filled with adventure, change, loss, and overcoming. Your relationship with papa's mom will grow and change. You will move to the warm, sunny desert that is Arizona instead of the chilly tundra of Alaska. You will leave your old friends to return in four or so years and make new ones. Papa will lose his battle with cancer in November of 2008, at which point his mom and family will disown you for a time. Just after papa passes away Grandma Mary will find out that she is facing a battle of her own with cancer and pass away only nine months later. You will struggle to find your new normal, however find strength in the strangest of places. You will be bullied at some point which will leave you confused. On the positive you will play soccer and start to learn to play the violin. You will change schools a few more times and among one of those changes you will find a violin teacher who will forever change your life.

2007 and 2008 will be difficult years however those challenges will be overcome. The challenges that you will face are much out of your realm of understanding being so young, however in the coming years you will come to understand the enormity of the challenges that you are facing in the current time. With papa's diagnosis you will initially be fearful because he will one day be almost entirely an outsider in your life and the next a fully-fledged parent. Christmas this year will be papa's last, you will spend it in Washington with Grandma Mary, papa and mommy. Only three days before Christmas mommy and papa will tell you that he not only has cancer, but it is terminal. Terminal is a fancy word meaning that he unfortunately will not survive his fight with cancer however what he is going through will help others in the future. You will find some comfort in understanding that. In the midst of papa's battle with cancer you will be moving to sunny Arizona instead of snowy Alaska with only two weeks to prepare to move to somewhere totally new. The blessing to moving to Arizona instead of Alaska is that you will be able to see papa more often and spend more time together because there is less distance between the two places.

Once you arrive in Arizona you will be surprised at how different your surroundings are compared to Washington. You will miss Washington and all of your friends, but be eager to learn more about your new surroundings and make new friends. In the fall you will start to play soccer, daddy will be the head coach of the team and papa will help out as much as he can while he is around. On November 24th he will pass away from cancer and due to threats that have been made by various members of papa's family and your own choice you will not attend any of the memorial or funeral services. Only three days after he passes away Grandma Mary, mom's mom will find out that she is also battling cancer. Hers is initially believed to be treatable and is until one of the chemo drugs that they gave her to cure the first cancer causes another to form. The second cancer that has formed will be untreatable and she will be able to visit Arizona once before she also loses her battle with cancer. After papa's passing his family will decide to disown you for a period of time that at the current moment you feel will be forever. For the first few months after his passing you wait for the phone call from at least one of them, but that phone call never comes. The fact they made the choice to push away is not your fault and neither is his passing even though you seem to think that at times. It's okay to feel that way, but allowing yourself to continue to grow is the best thing that you can do for you.

2009 will be a rollercoaster of a year. Grandma Mary will be cured of her cancer and then be re-diagnosed with cancer. The second time she is diagnosed she is given only months to live, hers is also terminal. By February you will begin taking violin lessons with a private teacher who will change your life. You will soon dedicate every ounce of effort into learning to play your instrument and make new friends in the process. 2009 will be the start of your second year in Arizona and you will transfer schools twice that year. You will also move on base and make more new friends. When grandma passes away you will again blame yourself, however know that it is not your fault. Cancer isn't something that you cause, they didn't pass away because you did anything wrong. Many of those around you in your peer group will start to view you differently and you will feel like an outsider. Don't let some mean bullies get you down because you are a bigger better person then they are. Remember to stay strong and keep your head up because life will get better.

-Older you

The Struggles of a Grieving Child

The time following my dad's passing is one that I one often go into detail about. It was a very low point in my life that I often try not to remember. Even thinking about it makes me want to believe that it didn't happen. With those feelings I have to remind myself of one thing. Now is the time to seize the opportunity that I have worked so hard to be given and write about it to inspire others so that they can work to overcome any challenge that they may be facing. This is the first fully exposed and honest look into what the process of grief was like for me at the age I was at the time. This can be what the process of grief is like for a young child. Every journey is and will be unique. This is mine.

    The day that my dad passed away was the day that I thought my world fell apart. I questioned why, how and when. Self-doubt coursed through my body. Others tried to comfort me. Despite their best efforts to convince me otherwise, I was convinced that I somehow caused his death. Guilt made it impossible or so I thought for me to get out of bed every morning. The reason that I got up in the morning was because papa did. His fighting spirit inspired me to wake up every morning. Since he was gone I thought that there was no reason to wake up and no purpose in life.

    As time went on the idea that he had passed away became easier to cope with. The anxiety, depression and grief on the other hand got worse. Though I had music and soccer to look forward to when I wasn't on the field or in the studio panic attacks often came out of the blue. They happened everywhere from the grocery store to at school with no obvious triggers. I remember feeling an overwhelming sense of paralyzing fear rush across my body. I could do nothing to make it better, no matter how hard I tried. I was often embarrassed when they happened thinking that I did something wrong to cause them.

My faith in God began to falter. I wondered if there was even a God why he would do such a thing to me. I ran from my faith and though I now believe in God, I have yet to return to my faith fully. I often considered ending my own life, though never actually planning to do so. Depression hit hard. So hard that for several years I was on and off anti-depressants. Nine months after my dad passed away, my mom's mom also passed away of the same evil disease. Though I wasn't all that close to my grandmother it was then that I came closest to potentially attempting suicide. I was done losing loved ones after the first loss of papa and his entire side of the family. After her passing I hit my lowest point. I was done. Or so I thought.

Thankfully my mom recognized the signs and kept me seeing a therapist. Despite my resistance she pushed on and I kept going. Had she not, I may not be alive today writing this. Though I had no plans of actually doing it, I did contemplate writing the note that no parent wants to receive. The therapist was able to convince me to want to move on. However, I still felt like I was at rock bottom. The bullying in 5th and 6th grade made my anxiety worse. They hospitalized me for over a week to make sure nothing else was wrong including a few days in a psych ward because someone that I thought I was close to wrongly claimed that I was suicidal.

After they realized the mistake they released me back to normal life. In 7th and 8th grade the bullying reached its peak. Though I loved my teachers and friends, by the third quarter of 7th grade it was decided that I would be doing school online until 8th grade. The decision wasn't an easy one, but after two death threats in a matter of months it was highly necessary. Homeschooling was a relief, but it gave me more time to think about my fears. By 8th grade I was back in public school still fearful, but better. Mid-year I was pulled out again until freshman year because of more threats.

In my 8th grade to freshman summer the same person as before wrongly told a therapist that I was suicidal. This time they tried to admit me to the psych ward straight away, but failed. I got so nervous that I almost stroked out. They sent me to the ER where doctors quickly set this person straight. They were explicitly told that I needed love and time to overcome my anxieties. Not a psych ward. Much to my surprise my freshman year was free of bullying for the most part. Though I would only be at the school for a year I made amazing friends. Before my sophomore year my family moved once again. Once I started at my new school I got bullied again. I took it for a few months. Then decided to finish high school at home and do my own thing.

Grief is a powerful emotion that can sometimes take years to overcome. To kids as young as I was feeling that grief can do unimaginable things. Without proper support, kids who lose a loved one can easily take a very wrong path. Had my mom not been so vigilant I don't know where I would have ended up or if I would even be here today. With proper support, kids like me can grow up to do amazing things. The key is along with proper support to treat them no different than their peers. Also educating their peers about what he or she has been through can help tremendously. As can pushing them to overcome their fears. Grief sucks, but it is possible to go from rock bottom to the top of your game. I am living proof of that. Will you be next?

Are We Even Family?

While my dad was here on earth, our family life seemed pretty normal. Even though my parents divorced when I was five, both sides of the family always made sure to include us in events or at least told us about them. The day that he passed changed everything with his family. We suddenly became outsiders within our own family. They began to distance themselves from us a few weeks after his passing. Eventually they stopped talking to us altogether for over fourteen months. At young age of ten it seemed as though one day we had a family to lean on and the next we didn't. Within a few days I went from grieving the loss of my father with his family behind me to grieving not only his death, but the loss of his entire family. I felt so incredibly defeated.

With their swift departure from our lives following his passing came guilt and depression. I often asked my mom what I did wrong to make them leave. No matter how much she reassured me that I did nothing, I refused to believe it. Getting out of bed every morning was a struggle. I became unsure of my purpose on this earth or if I even had one. I lived in constant guilt, sadness and uncertainty. Following his passing, his family (his mom and one sister) took absolutely everything of his which made my levels of guilt and grief skyrocket. The one thing that they didn't have was his handprint. He made those in Arizona for only my sister and me.

After fourteen months of no contact with his family. I decided to reach out to them with my mom's blessing. I called my grandmother and one aunt. Neither of them answered at first. Both eventually called back. Though I was thrilled, I was also weary that there would be eventual rejection. They both seemed genuinely excited but in the moment I failed to realize one thing. Instead of talking about the past and trying to re-include us in the family they seemed to conveniently forget to discuss the past year and mentioned nothing about anyone but themselves in the current time.

After a few months of phone conversations, some more difficult than others Grandma Elizabeth, Aunt Portia and Katelynn surprised us with a visit in May of 2010. The visit was a blur of excitement, forgiveness and confusion. The first week our aunt and cousin were also there. After that week, they went home and it was just our family and Grandma. We enjoyed some time with just her. We showed her some of the very few memories that papa brought with him during his visits. All went well until we brought out the handprints that were made by him for only Marissa and me. Grandma seemed awestruck initially. Then once she realized that there were only two, I felt a sense of spiteful jealousy. The rest of the visit following showing her the handprints went well, though I could still feel some tension in the air.

Over the next several years, significant progress was made including another visit. However, when we weren't together it seemed like no one cared about us being a part of the family. We were never told about graduations, deaths or family functions. The times when we did find out, it was after the fact with a claim that we couldn't go to them. Reasoning for us "not being able to make it" often included us not caring, us not living in state or somehow we were "forgotten" about. When I was younger it hurt me more than it does now. When all of this occurred to me, feelings of us somehow being in the wrong and resentment came to the surface. I felt as though I longed for a family that I would never have.

Fast forward a few years and you end up in November of 2014 when we decided that we were headed to Michigan for the first time in over half a decade. Papa's family seemed excited, yet hesitant for some reason. Almost as if they felt that we would do something wrong. All that we asked of them prior to our visit was for his ashes. Which they had wrongfully kept since the day that he passed in 2008... Over six years. Although we didn't force the issue of them giving us his ashes before we left. Rightfully so we strongly encouraged it. On the week we went to Michigan the days fell in the order that they did the year that he passed away.

By the end of that nine-day visit, significant progress had been made. On December 1, 2014, the night before we were supposed to leave Grandma Elizabeth, brought us a long overdue surprise. Papa's ashes. We were so thrilled and grateful that she gave them to us, because we began to doubt that she actually would. In the moment, though it was beautiful we failed to realize one thing. She had given us some of them, but not everything that we were supposed to get. After she gave them to us, we had to figure out how to get him home with us. It was decided that I would be the one to carry papa's ashes home in my backpack.

Over the next year our relationship with them fluctuated from slightly frayed to as close to normal as it could get. Nearly exactly one year after we found out that we were headed to Michigan for the first time in so long. I found out that I would be going to the Midwest for a college visit. On the final day of that visit I would be driving eight hours roundtrip to and from Michigan to visit them. Aunt Portia and Grandma Elizabeth both seemed excited and said that they wanted to meet up. I was excited to take the trip, but knew that I would be exhausted afterwards.

In the planning of this trip I realized that I would be seeing her on December 1st. Exactly one year to the day after she gave us papa's ashes. As a thank you, I decided to draw her an angel and bring it with me to give to her. She seemed genuinely surprised and grateful that I thought of bringing her another angel. Before I knew it I had been back in Washington for a week or two. I decided to ask her where she had put the angel. Her answer shook me to the core.

She said that papa was now too small to put it next to him. I remember internally pausing, trying not to make it obvious over the phone. I was so disappointed. I asked her who else had part of his ashes. Her answer was one that I expected, but hoped wasn't true. She said that Aunt Portia who I am close with and "Auntie" Brie, my abuser had some. I had been lied to... again. When papa passed he wanted to be split into four parts, one big one to stay at my mom's house and three little ones. One for his mom, one for Marissa and one for me. During that moment of utter betrayal. I almost slipped a secret that I wasn't ready to tell them. That I was sexually abused.

When I did eventually tell them Aunt Portia's reaction was that of sorrow and support. My grandmother almost refused to believe me. It seems as though she loves my abuser even more now. In her presence I pretend that it doesn't bother me. When in reality it sickens me to the core. So are we even family? I guess it depends on how you view family. I love all of them dearly, however sometimes they treat my sister and I like outsiders. At times I don't even feel as though we are related. I guess that definition continues to change as time goes on. For now, as long as everyone remains fully honest, I see a bright future. If not, I see something else. Either way I am fine with the outcome because I am fine with being me. That being said, the ball is now in their court. Are we even family?

Answer: I don't know it's now up to them to decide.

Love Rewritten

On the morning of November 24, 2008 my father James Anthony Gorski lost his courageous year-long battle with cancer at the age of only 42. He was a man of great character, who loved his family and friends more than anything. He loved to play games with my sister Marissa and me as well as our mom. Though they have been divorced for a few years now and my mom is remarried our broken family became one over this past year. We will always remember him for his smile and presence in a room. Most of his friends knew him for his younger years on the soccer field. As the goal keeper with the bright red hat.

    Aside from being an amazing father, husband and friend he was also a cherished son, little brother, uncle, cousin and godfather to many. He took pride in everything that he set out to accomplish and tried to make an impact wherever he went. At family gatherings, he was the life of the party. There was never a dull moment when he was around. Out of his many titles, the ones that he took the most pride in were father, husband, son and little brother. He was often a selfless man who put the needs of others before his own. In his passing he hoped that people would celebrate his life and cherish his "wife", kids and family instead of mourning his passing.

    He is survived by his two young children Alana (me) age 10 and Marissa age 8 and our mother Valerie. Also his parents Elizabeth and George, his sisters and several nieces, nephews, cousins and friends. Services will be held in the summer of 2012 or 2016 at St. Andrew Catholic Church in Rochester Michigan. There will be a small service in his honor at that same church on Sunday December 7, 2008 in his honor. Instead of flowers, we ask that you bring a monetary donation to Tu Nidito Family services in Tucson Arizona. They helped us through the past year and gave him peace knowing we are loved.

Love of Daughters

Nearly eight years ago on the morning of November 24, 2008. My sister Marissa and I lost our knight in shining armor. Now instead of armor, he wears angel wings and watches over us from above instead of here on earth. When I think of the man that he was to not only my mom, sister and I, but to all of you as his friends and family I am awe inspired. Though he was far from perfect, he always did his best at everything that he set out to accomplish. He loved with his full heart and was determined to help others each and every day.

Growing up wasn't easy from about 2005 to 2007. Essentially from the time that my mom was forced to divorce him until his cancer diagnosis it seemed like we barely knew each other at times because we lived in different states. When we did visit, abuse ensued behind his back or while he was at work. This lead to high amounts of distrust and some fear of being around him. Through the hard times there were some positive memories. However, the person that I remember the most is the father that he became following his diagnosis. The father I only had eleven short months to get to know.

In that year, I came to know the father that I had longed for since I was young. I remember seeing him exude so much joy when we did the smallest things such as play and win a soccer game. When I would play the violin or Marissa would sing and being able to send us off to school every morning. During that year our once broken family became one. My mom, sister and I welcomed him into our home and hearts, free of judgment or hard feelings. Though still geographically separated by hundreds of miles. He religiously made the drive from southern California to visit us in southern Arizona every month between treatments.

In Arizona he helped my stepdad coach our undefeated U-12 soccer team. The team loved and respected him like he was our full time head coach. Initially he was shy about critiquing us fearing he would overstep a boundary. My stepdad quickly made it very clear that papa was as much of a coach as he was. Papa's opinion was valuable as they were both trained a similar way. It was a natural choice for him to help coach us. On occasion papa even took charge and ran practice if my stepdad couldn't. Like my stepdad he demanded total respect and pushed us to our limits each and every practice. Often making critiques over the small details, claiming that they made the difference. Papa was very critical, but always fair. He made every decision with our best interest in mind.

The times that weren't spent on the soccer field, at school or practicing music were usually spent doing the simple things. We loved to cook together, read, draw and do crafts. One of my favorite things that we did together was make the infamous handprints. Though I was timid about getting close to him I did treasure each memory that we made together. He often made it a point to tell Marissa and me how beautiful and talented we were. He pointed out how much he loved Marissa's imaginative stories and drawings as well as my poetry and knack for writing narratives. One thing that I did tell him was that I wanted to be an author and share my story with the world one day. He encouraged me to go for it simply stating that I would know when the right time came. Same with Marissa's dream of being a pop star and a detective or a ninja, if I remember correctly.

Papa often made sure to tell us to follow our dreams no matter what anyone tells us is or is not possible. His biggest dream of having a wife and kids was fulfilled. Despite him and my mom's divorce, he never stopped loving her with his full heart. Making sure to remind us of that daily. The treatments that he did for his cancer were mostly clinical trials. He knew that they wouldn't change his outcome because he was terminal. The results however would change the lives of countless others. Knowing that he was directly impacting the lives of others gave him the courage to fight every day. Though he was courageous, every knight in shining armor has their fears. His were of us hating him or forgetting who he was. To aid him I overcoming those fears and help us with our own grief. As a family we went to support groups at Tu Nidito family services in Tucson Arizona.

On November 23, 2008, the day before he passed away I did something that I hadn't done before. I opened up to him about my fears of his diagnosis and the memories that we had made since then. The conversation was mostly a blur. I do however remember a few distinct details. I thanked him for being my father. I told him that I was afraid for the day that he passed away and laid out my life's plan to him. It was a conversation filled with laughter, gratitude and tears. Almost like I knew on some strange way that time was incredibly limited. On that day he also talked to his oldest sister Aunt Portia for the first time in two years. He opened up to her as much as he could. It was their first conversation in a long time, and it ended up being their last.

In the years following his passing life wasn't always easy, but it was meaningful. Grief is no joke, which is why it took so long for this distant dream to become reality. Marissa and I have handled grief in different ways. We have overcome even the hardest times in our own ways and become better, stronger people because of it. Marissa is now sixteen and wants to one day serve our country and join the military. I am now eighteen and my dream of becoming an author has come true. For Marissa the understanding of grief and the finality of death came as she grew older. At the time of his passing she was too young to understand either. That being said, I was old enough to understand both and went through this process at a much younger age.

"It is now my honor to speak on behalf of both of us. We are both eternally grateful that you all made it out here today. Thank you so much for loving and remembering him like we do. Also for understanding and giving us time to properly grieve and move on. As well as grow up free of worry about being judged. We now ask that instead of mourning his passing. You celebrate the life that he lived, cherishing only the positive memories that you had with him. We will forever love and remember him, but we will move in and celebrate his joyous life. Once again. On behalf of both of us. Thank you so much for coming. Blessings to all."

James Anthony Gorski

March 5, 1966-November 24, 2008

The Unthinkable Answer

A question that people often ask me is "What is it like losing a parent at such a young age?" When I was younger I took that question as almost an insult. Not because anyone asked it condescendingly, but because I was unable to understand why the question was being asked. To me not having my dad around was normal after a while. Now I realize that the question of what it's like losing a parent at a young age is an opportunity to share and explain a part of life that would ne inconceivable to most. My answer is usually something like this...

Imagine being only nine years old when, the world is just barely coming into focus and being told that your dad has one year or less left on this earth. You live on pins and needles. You fear that every phone call from his number is the one that you expect eventually, yet dread. You realize that no one is perfect, not even your knight in shining armor. This leads to forgiveness of all wrongdoings. You say everything that you ever wanted to tell him because each day that goes by is one day closer to not being able to say anything at all. You live in constant fear of immediate change.

When that phone call comes, your world instantly falls apart. You realize that you are now different from everyone else. Papa will never be the goofy dad who embarrasses me before sending me off to homecoming or prom. He will never see me graduate high school or college. He will never meet the man that I will eventually call my husband. I will never have the opportunity to see his face when I am ready to start a new chapter in life.

Despite all that he will miss I don't feel envious of those who have both parents alive. I was given the gift of knowing that he loves me. That's all I need. I would rather have him free of suffering then have had more time. I miss him every day, but I do my best to make him proud, honor his legacy and be grateful for what I do have. I will always love him but in some ways his passing was a blessing. I learned the lesson of taking nothing for granted and enjoying each day no matter what challenges are put in my path to face. All one needs to know is that each challenge is a lesson meant to be learned.

Loss in a Young Life

As a writer it is up to me to bring every story that I choose to tell to life. Sometimes the inspiration to tell those stories comes naturally within a few hours or minutes. While the inspiration to tell others takes months or even years of thought and searching to find the right words to properly depict. This story in particular is one that I have wanted to tell for many years, but the inspiration just never came. That is until I heard a song called "Roses and Violets" by Alexander Jean. I first heard the song on November 24, 2015, the day that marked 7 years since my dad passed away. Hearing it immediately inspired a story in me that I still couldn't find the words to explain. Even though the words were still lost, I could see the story coming to life. After a few months of listening to the song several times and thinking about a few different stories I realized that it depicted the story of the year plus following my dad's passing, a time when we had no contact with his family and the journey leading up to it. I chose to write it as a letter to his mother because to me letters are the best way to understand a journey between two people on an in depth level.

Dear Grandma Elizabeth,

On December 22, 2007 my mom and papa sat us down and told us that he had terminal cancer. Although they had been divorced for a few years at the time and my mom was happily remarried to the man who has raised me since age five they all agreed that with his diagnosis we would all become one family until the day that he passed away. We all grew closer over his eleven-month fight with cancer. We were able to say our goodbyes, come to an understanding about what the future would look like after he passed and say everything that we wanted to tell him. Although he lived in Southern California and we lived in Western Washington and moved to Southern Arizona in March of 2008, we tried to spend as much time together as we could. He would come out to visit on a monthly basis between treatments. While he was with us he fit right into our everyday life. For the first time in my life I was able to see who he truly was as a person and treasure the memories of him just being a parent. One of my favorite things that we did together was when he put his handprints in plaster and wrote messages to my sister and me on them once they hardened. To this day that handprint is one of my most treasured possessions.

    Although he would come to visit us often during the time he was in California, other then what he told us on the phone his life there and his relationships with you and his sisters were a mystery to us. Until the day that he passed away we had no idea that he had only told our family and the sister that he lived with that his cancer was terminal. On the day he passed, November 24, 2008 my mom got a brief phone call that said "Jim's dead" from his phone and then ended from who we believe to have been the sister he lived with. Without thinking my mom called you in a panic not knowing if it was true or not and trying to identify the origin of that phone call. It turns out that she unintentionally told you that he had passed away. After that phone call, it being confirmed to be true and a few rather harsh phone calls from one of his sisters we had no contact with any of you for over fourteen months. Prior to his passing we knew that you could potentially take it extremely harshly, feel that the world was out to get you and push us out of your life for a period of time or permanently. We had hoped that the outcome would be the opposite and that you would be able look to us for support. Unfortunately, our worst fears came true.

Although initially we hoped that after a week or two you would come around, we quickly realized that it would be a very long time before we saw or spoke to you again. During the first year after his passing I constantly thought about how much I wished that we could be going through the process of grief together. I felt like I wasn't good enough to be a part of your life. During the eleven months that papa had cancer my tattered relationship with you had grown so close. Then as soon as he passed it was as if none of the work we had done with our relationship mattered. It seemed like someone had come in with a wrecking ball and tore down everything that we had built as far as the relationship between you and I went. It was like losing an entire family in one day. I was done saying goodbye and hoped that my gut feeling of us one day being reunited would become a reality. With you living across the country in the Midwest not seeing each other on a regular basis wasn't unusual. However, not having any phone contact with you was difficult.

During the year that we had no contact, I tried to remind myself that distance makes the heart grow. Also that you needed time to grow as a person and so did I. It seemed as if you could only see the light of day when he was around. Not realizing or allowing yourself to see that he was in your heart the entire time. It seemed like the day he passed your life fell apart. I could do nothing even though all I wanted to do was fix it. I hoped that you would learn that love is truly blind and how to enjoy life again. I also hoped that you would realize that sometimes love isn't enough to bring someone back no matter how much you wish they could come back eventually accepting that loving him whether he is here or not is all that you can do.

After slightly over a year with my parents' blessing I decided to reach out. As I was calling, I was shaking because I was so nervous. I hoped that you would accept me and not turn your back again. If I remember correctly, you didn't answer. Which made the possibility of you turning your back again seem all the more real. Even though my heart sank, I reminded myself to stay calm and left a voice mail, praying to God that you would call back. A few days later you did call back. I was so beyond excited to hear your voice again after so long and have a chance at a relationship in the future. I am so proud that you took the chance and accepted me again. By doing that you made my one wish when he passed come true.

Love,

Alana G.

It has taken time but I am happy to say that today about 5 years later we are still in regular contact, have seen each other a few times and are continuing to grow our relationship. She needed time to grow and so did I. I realize that the time that we spent apart made us grow into better, stronger people. Even though I still don't agree with the way she handled things back then, I realize that we all grieve differently. I feel content knowing I can't change the past and that we were meant to have a relationship and grow together. Love is truly unconditional and as long as we both continue to understand that I can see nothing but a bright future with her and I having contact.

Papa's Message

When I think of my father who passed away when I was ten at the age of 42; the three words that instantly come to mind are humility, grace and forgiveness. He wasn't always perfect. In fact, from the time my sister was three and I was five until she was seven and I was nine when he was essentially given a death sentence in the form of terminal cancer he was barely even a parent. During the four years that he was only in our lives when we would go to visit him he felt more like an uncle. For two of those four years my mom, sister and I lived with her husband in Washington while he lived in California with his sister. During our visits to California that lasted anywhere from one to six or eight weeks, chaos and abuse ensued. His lifestyle was a busy party boy, almost bachelor like lifestyle that was always on the go in a suburban city in California. Which was a stark contrast to our structured, yet laid back family like lifestyle in a sleepy town in Washington. Going there was almost like being dropped into one of those round cages at the circus that dirt bikes ride around in with no way to get out. There was constant noise confusion with almost a threatening vibe in the air 24/7 that was I remember to be incredibly unsettling. While we were there we were physically, verbally and sexually abused by his sister, brother in law and a cousin. We were threatened with harm should we tell anyone. As with most abusers, they only did it when he wasn't around leaving no trail of evidence. With the exception of a few drunken rages, or should I say idiosyncrasies he never knew about any of it or would have believed us had we told him.

In November of 2007 the equivalent of an atom bomb was dropped on him in the form of a terminal cancer diagnosis. When he called to tell my mom she nearly hung up on him because she was so fed up with what was happening while we were visiting. She was only days away from putting a restraining order on him and fighting to take his visitation rights away forever. When she realized that he was serious and not just pulling her leg to get his visitation rights back she, Paco and my papa collectively decided to open up a path and work towards forgiveness. My mom and papa told us on December 22, 2007 told us about his cancer in our sleepy town in Washington while my stepdad was overseas on military duty. My grandmother on my mom's side (Grandma Mary) was also living with us at the time. At the moment that we were told about papa's cancer, they explained their decision. Marissa and I decided to agree with them and work towards forgiveness. Shortly after finding out about papa's cancer diagnosis I remember being afraid to love him because I knew that he would soon be gone. I was willing to and did forgive him. I also intently listened to him as he explained and apologized for his downfalls. Especially for not believing us when we told him that things weren't okay, even then I was afraid to get attached or open up to him.

    Despite my fearful resistance, he never gave up trying. Papa would calmly talk to me even if I was afraid to get too close when he would visit and over the phone had the same calm but determined voice. It took over eleven months of him trying before I eventually opened up. Little did I know that the day that I opened up would be his last full day here on this earth. Although I remember that I opened up, I have very few clear memories of exactly the words that were spoken in our final hour or so long conversation. A few years ago, my mom told me that after I was finished talking to him for what would be the last time, when I handed her the phone he was in tears. His first words to her were "she finally opened up to me". Papa then went on to tell her how grateful that his persistence with me had paid off. Most importantly he was grateful I didn't hate him. I love you Papa. You were everything that I ever wished for in a dad and know that you love me. Our last conversation is a memory I will forever cherish. He was my knight in shining armor and always will be. It only took one conversation to change everything. It's never too late to make change.

Your Life Story

Sometimes I what you would think of the person I am today.

If you are proud of the things that I have accomplished.

If you support the decisions that I have made.

Sometimes I wonder if I look more like you or mom.

If my features more closely resemble yours or hers.

If my personality is more similar to yours or hers

Sometimes I wonder about the memories that you and mom shared

What hearing about those times from you would be like

If there is anything that you and her had always dreamt of telling us together

If there is anything that I still don't know about those times

Sometimes I wonder what you were like growing up

If you were a wild child or a wall flower

If you always knew that you wanted to have a family

Sometimes I wonder why things played out the way they did

Why you passed away when you were so young

Then I realize that your passing was simply a lesson.

One that helped me find the courage to speak out and share my story

I will forever miss you, however I know that I cannot allow grief to control the path that I will take

I need to move forward from those feelings, work towards my goals and pursue my passions

Most importantly allowing myself to understand that wondering about you is only natural.

Fly Baby Bird

November 28th is a day that I now know has great meaning to who I am. On that day in 1998 I was welcomed into God's kingdom and into the Catholic Church through the sacred sacrament of baptism. On that very day exactly seventeen years later I set out into this amazing world on my own for the very first time. On that day in 1998 both of my parents were physically present, in 2015 it was only my mom who was there to see me off, however I did have a little something that reminded me of him with me. Packing for my first solo journey was bitter sweet because every other trip that I had been on I had been with my mom and sister, the thought of not having them there was saddening. Some even thought that I was crazy or wouldn't make it on the plane. In the past even going to a friend's house to spend the night has been challenging. So when I decided to go half way across the country on my own for 4 nights and 5 days I was nervous but determined to make it happened. It also helped that I only had a few days to think about it.

When the day came I was so nervous, at times throughout the day I was unsure if I would even make it on the plane to be totally honest. I have had anxiety that has varied in severity for over a decade, I was trying to push all of the nervous thoughts out of my head and enjoy everything that was going on. I would be traveling from Seattle, Washington to Chicago, Illinois via plane and then driving about an hour to Indiana where I would be staying with my stepdad dad and his dad for the time that I was there. I would also be taking one day to travel about eight hours roundtrip to and from Michigan to visit family. Prior to setting out on this adventure while still in the planning phases I at times thought that I was crazy for deciding to go on this trip. Once I got there I would hit the ground running in a place that I had never really been before and have to take everything as it came. We had planned everything down to the minute and I knew that there wasn't room for error, should something run even a hair late it could cause me to miss my flight home.

By the time that we were ready to leave for the airport I was more determined than ever, I had a goal in mind and there was nothing that would stop me from reaching it. Even at that point as my mom stepdad and me were driving to the airport I thought that I was ready but it really didn't hit me until my stepdad and I said adios to my mom at the airport and watched her drive away. Instantly everything became real then got even more real once we were through security. I tried to stay calm, we were catching a later flight out of Seattle so we had time to eat dinner before we took off, the only sign of how nervous and excited I felt was that I didn't eat much until we got on the plane when the nerves subsided slightly. As we were taking off I was almost questioning if I had made the correct decision, however there was no turning back at that point and I realized that the only thing that I could do was be excited for what was ahead. After over a four-hour flight from Seattle to Chicago and a one-hour drive from Chicago we had made it to Northwest Indiana. Even though it was two in the morning on Sunday at that point I was so excited to meet my grandfather for the first time in eleven years who stayed awake until we arrived safely. After we arrived we all went to bed after a very long first day. Baby bird had spread her wings.

The next few days flew by. On Sunday we went shopping to purchase a frame for a very special angel that I had drawn for my grandmother in Michigan to be delivered on Tuesday. Next we went to East Chicago, Indiana to get Mexican cookies and pastries that reminded me of when we lived in Arizona. On the drive there I was able to get my first glimpse of my surroundings and see the University campus that I would be shadowing my stepdad at the next day in Indiana. It felt so surreal, actually being on a University campus is something that I have hoped to be able to do since I first decided that I truly wanted to pursue a career in aviation when I was fourteen. At that moment I understood how privileged that I was to have been given the opportunity to go on this trip. After we left campus and the bakery we realized that I had forgotten something quite important, a winter coat, so we went out and purchased one. Once all of that was over and got back to my grandfather's house it was time to meet more people. I met a great aunt and uncle and a third cousin. By the end of the second day I was exhausted and wanted time to go by slower. I realized that although it was different being away from my mom and sister I was enjoying it. I missed them and wished that they could be there however my nerves were gone.

      Day three was a dream come true, I was not only able to visit my dream school, I was also able to have a day in the life of a student there. The classes seemed longer then what I was used to when I was in public school but compared to homeschooling they felt average. After each of the three classes I went to I was able to talk to the professor that taught them and receive valuable information about getting into Purdue and how to go about choosing the right college for me. I was also able to talk to a few students between classes and hear their perspectives on student life, workload and how and when to declare a major. By the end of the day I had come to a definite conclusion that Purdue was my school, without a doubt being able to shadow someone who went there made the decision much easier. By the end of the day I felt as if I needed time to reflect. On the way from school to my grandfather's house my stepdad and I were discussing the trip to Michigan that we would be taking the next day to see some family and friends while I was in town, also to hand deliver my angel to its new home. I was excited but knew that the 36 hours would be chaotic. Day 4 would be 8 hours and 400+ miles of travel by car with an early morning and late night which would flow into day 5 catching an 8AM flight out of Chicago.

Day four started before the sun was even up. My stepdad and I were up at 5AM to hit the road at 6 and at that moment I thought I was crazy. Three time zone changes and over 2,000 miles in the next thirty hours. Once we hit the road I was able to see the beauty of the Midwest. A region that although I was born there I have seen very little of. Being late fall all of the trees were bare and once we crossed the border of Michigan all that you could see for miles was farmland. After about four hours on the road we had reached our destination just outside of Detroit. Although my visit was short we tried to make the most out of the time that we had together. The first mission that I had to accomplish while visiting Michigan was to give the angel to its new owner, my grandmother who exactly one-year prior had given my family my biological father's ashes. On that day she gave us her angel and one year later I was able to bring her a new one. While I was there we also saw one of my aunts, some friends and my grandfather who was recovering from surgery in the hospital. Although my visit was brief lifelong memories were made. Once we arrived back in Indiana around 10PM it was time to pack and say farewell to my grandfather who I had grown close too while I was visiting.

Day 5 started early and much to my surprise it was snowing! Unfortunately, it was dark so I wasn't able to enjoy it as much. Driving to the airport was saddening. Prior to leaving for Indiana I thought that I may be excited to return home and I was, however I wished that I had more time to have spent there. I had just formed so many relationships and to have to say farewell for now so soon after was saddening. Despite the profound sadness there was some banter between myself and my stepdad about if my flight would be delayed or not. Once we arrived at the airport in Chicago the nerves hit once again. This time they were subtle, but present, this would be my first ever flight truly alone. Thankfully he was allowed to walk me to the gate and stay with me until we took off. After boarding the flight, we sat at the gate for over 40 minutes because of the snow. I won the bet which was oddly satisfying.

    At takeoff the nerves went away and turned into pride. During the flight I took photos of the ground below, watched movies and wrote a bit. The past few days had flown by I was so excited to be returning home, but missed Indiana already. I couldn't wait to tell my mom and sister about my trip. As we were approaching the airport in Seattle we flew low enough to clearly see the ground below. Although it was a cool gloomy day we were still able to see the dazzling city skyline and the trees for miles. As soon as we landed I realized that I had made it. I had proved all of the doubters wrong. I can be in this world and just be me. Things that one or two years prior would have been impossible I was able to do. Baby bird had landed and grown in the process. Anxiety did not win this time, I did and I couldn't be happier that I set out with a goal and achieved it by taking that trip. I now know that my internal strength is far greater than even I know.

The Set Up for Success

Sometimes I look in the mirror and see that frightened but excited girl who walked into my first practice on the YMCA swim team over two years ago. Yet other times I see someone who looks a decade older than I did at that time. Without the foundation of swimming at the YMCA that summer I would have never had the chance to find myself until much later in life if ever. It took the two coaches who saw me swimming on my own with the coaching of my mom to invite me to join the team, to believe in me from the beginning even when I didn't believe in myself. They came in early on days that we didn't have practice to work with me and never gave up. Even though I only swam for them for one season, I feel that they set the foundation for me to become who I am today. They encouraged me to be confident and not be afraid to take chances. Without them I wouldn't have had the chance at any sort of swim career, have been willing to take chances both on the deck and off and become confident in my own skin. They may never see this or know how much they impacted me. However, they forever changed my life in the few months that I swam for them and I am eternally grateful for that.

Success Despite Resistance

   Along this journey thus far some of my most profound doubters have been family members. Mainly on my father's side, they have repeatedly expressed their lack of support for my message and the fact that I am coming out and sharing my story. However, despite their lack of support and doubt I have decided to move forward with doing so anyways. With the doubt and displeasure that they have been expressing I have naturally wondered why. There is a saying out there that says that you are only as sick as your darkest secret, I have often pondered upon the thought behind that saying and if the reason that they don't want this to succeed is because there is a bigger secret in the family then even I know. I have asked them often what is wrong with me opening up about my journey, they often respond with something such as me shedding dirt upon the family for no reason. What dirt am I shedding on anyone by opening up about my personal life?

   One thing I have learned throughout their expressions of doubt is to not listen to the doubters because they are often the ones with something to hide. If you have a dream, don't be afraid to afraid to try to reach it. There may be bumps in the road to getting there, however as long as you keep giving 100% effort and don't give up anything is possible.

Dear Willow

Dear Willow,

I remember you a vibrant and intelligent little two and three-year-old. You were like a sister to me and my sister Marissa when we would visit our dad in California. I know that your memories of us are likely fleeting. If they even exist at all, they are probably pretty vague. However, mine of you are as clear as day. The last time we saw each other was a tumultuous park visit in 2008 when you were four, Marissa was eight and I was only ten. We were there visiting from Arizona so that the adults could discuss what they would all do when papa aka Uncle Jimbo eventually passed away or his health declined. Although we were only at that park for an hour or so and the adults got into a verbal tiff spending time with you was a light in the darkness just like it had been before. The last time we talked on the phone was likely just days before papa/your Uncle Jimbo passed away in November of 2008.

You always had something witty to say and almost always had wild hair. Wild to the point that Uncle Jimbo called you Phyllis after the famous comedian Phyllis Diller. From the beginning he loved you more than you will ever know, like you were his own. I know with full confidence that he is proud of the young lady that you have become. While we were in California visiting him, life wasn't always easy. In fact, there was often abuse and hate flying around usually aimed at me by all of the adults in the house except papa. I have prayed every day since the last time I saw you for your safety and happiness. That you were spared from the abuse, pain and fear that I went through. Having stated that, I do have realistic expectations and am fully aware that you may have been or are being abused if you are being, have been or question that you may have been or are being abused. It's okay to get help and ask those questions.

Some of my favorite memories of spending time together are the times that papa would take us to Huntington Beach. We would build sand castles in the hot sun and body surf in the cool waves all day long. Always ending up seemingly wearing the beach in our clothing by the time the day was over. Often times we would pick up seashells and sand and put them in the dried out and emptied drink bottles that he would give us with our names on them. So they wouldn't get lost. After the days on the beach drew to a close papa would take all of us (usually Tiffany, Marissa, you and me) to dinner at the restaurant on the peer. After dinner was over we would head back to the house, shower off and tuck in for the night.

Most days during the week were spent around the house with a nanny, Tiffany or on the rare occasion just Aunt Brie. That is unless papa or your dad brought us to work with them. The days around the house were typically long and sometimes filled with abuse that you were too young to remember. There were some moments of joy. On those joyous days spent around the house. There was always a looming fear that something bad could happen. When something bad did happen, I always did the best that I could to keep you, Marissa and Sydney safe. Even during the times when Tiffany failed to do so or wasn't around. No matter how dark things were sometimes, your light was always brighter.

In all honesty, you probably saved my life in more ways than one with your contagious joy. Had you not been around those days likely would have felt as dark as they actually were. Another part of what I remember helped me get through those dark days is the bond between you, Marissa and me. A bond that is and was indescribably amazing and something that I still carry with me to this day and forever will. During our visits to California you, Marissa and me did everything together, partly because out of your siblings, only you lived with your parents full time and also because we loved each other so incredibly much.

The days that papa and or your dad would take all of us to work with them were treasured. It was on those days filled with quality time spent together that we were able to just able to treasure being a kid. On those days that were sometimes few and far between, the chance of abuse ensuing was extremely low. We made lifelong memories running around the office together like a bunch of sneaky wild clowns, drew pictures, played with the copier and went to job sites with the guys. You loved being sneaky and often played little pranks on people. So when you were taken to work by someone you climbed into a cabinet on someone's desk and popped out when they walked in. You also locked your dad out of his office and truck and took the keys…Multiple times. Frankly he's lucky that you always kept them and didn't throw them out or flush them down the toilet. I remember one time when one your dad's employees asked you what you wanted to be when you grew up. Your answer: one of the guys.

Going out in public with you at that age was quite an adventure. Sometimes the fun started before we even arrived at our destination. By the time you were about two, you figured out how to unbuckle yourself and break free of your car seat. You often did this with horrendous timing. Your favorite time to do it was on the freeway, in traffic, where it was impossible to pull over. After someone finally got you back into your car seat and we arrived at our destination, the real fun started. For some odd reason you enjoyed walking up to random strangers and explicitly telling them that your mom was a bitch. After a while of you doing this and getting blamed for your language papa gave up telling you to knock it off and telling people that you weren't his kid. You said such a thing at grocery stores, malls and airports to name a few places. You also used to tell them that you loved us, papa, Tiffany and our mom who you called mom.

When we weren't in California we would talk to each other often. Almost always on papa's phone which you had either stolen and called us on or he had given to you. Most of the time you wanted to talk to "mom" first, then you would ask for Marissa or me. I distinctly recall hearing you tell me that you loved me and asked me when we were coming to see you next. Up until late 2007 when he got diagnosed with terminal cancer, I always knew. After his diagnosis I didn't, but wished more than anything that I could tell you. Nine years later I still don't know the answer to that question. However, my faith is stronger than ever and I fully believe that one day there will be an answer and we will reunite.

Until then I will continue to pray for your safety every day and hold onto the hope that you know who your Uncle Jim is. He loved you so very much and still does to this day even though he isn't physically here. He practically raised you until the day he passed and was happy to do so. I miss you every day and as this book came to be. I knew that a letter to you had to be in it. Know that you are loved and missed every day. I can hardly believe that I am penning this letter eight years after we last saw each other. I am now nearly eighteen and you are going into middle school. There is so much more that I wanted to say, but the words I didn't write are better spoken. I hope that one day you will read this so I can answer any questions you may have. We will reunite one day. I love you with all my heart and so does Marissa.

Until Next Time with Love

-Your cousin Alana.

The Unseen Sacrifice

As a military family the sacrifices we all made were split. There are some sacrifices that we all see each other make such as the times when he worked long hours, moving and when he had to go away on a deployment or to train aka (TDY). When he would go away on a deployment or TDY after he left the gate at the airport our worlds became separate, we couldn't be with him and see what his world looked like and nor could he with ours. He didn't see the tears that we cried at night or the struggle that my mom had during the first weeks or month of his deployment. We didn't feel the terror that must have jolted through him as he was touching down in a warzone or hear mortars or gunshots on a daily basis. Despite the sacrifices that we all made, we learned to get excited over the smallest victories and celebrate the smallest milestones that we reached while he was deployed. When he came home we would rejoice and enjoy the time that we had together after.

I was a proud military brat from the day that my mom married my stepdad when I was six years old until the day that he retired when I was fourteen. That being said I went through the usual litany of deployments, moves and so on and so forth. It was normal for me to see my dad to work wearing a uniform, deploy and move around every few years however my normal would change the day that he decided to retire. On that day we were looking at one final move, this time to a familiar place. We would be moving back to the Pacific Northwest, this time instead of making new friends I would be trying to reconnect with old ones. None of whom I had seen since the day that I left Washington. I hoped that they would remember me, one day when I left we were all in 4th grade and when I came back we were in high school.

After my stepdad left the military it seemed as though he had gotten lost in the civilian world. It seemed like his PTSD or post-traumatic stress disorder was dormant until he left the military. After his career had ended he transformed into a different person. Something that isn't as uncommon as you may think, often times after men and women leave the military they feel lost in society. Flash backs started and got worse and worse, then turned into fits of rage. He seemed to constantly be back in that mindset of self-defense and self-preservation the same state of mind that he was in while he was deployed. For over twenty years he was thought to think one way and do any one thing one way, after so many years of repeating those teachings they don't just go away overnight.

Sometimes when this happens forcing your family member to go out on their own is the best way for them to heal from these wounds. In my specific situation one day in January of 2015 when one of his fits of rage became too much, my mom forced him to leave. This may seem harsh however it is often times the best thing for them. In his case he admittedly needed that swift kick in the pants because had she not kicked him out and isolated he would have never gotten help. While he was in our home for whatever reason he felt as if getting help would make him less of a person. We didn't talk to him for over five months after he was kicked out for the simple reason of his PTSD not allowing him to think of anyone but himself. In the military the mindset was self-preservation. Isolating him allowed him to see what it was like without the support system of a family. Something that he was grateful for, however at times took for granted while he was in the military.

We are currently at a standstill. The fate of our family remaining one is uncertain. My mom, sister and I have done our best to help him. Now it's up to my stepdad to try.

Dear Paco

Dear Paco,

      Though you raised me from the ages of five to about fifteen, my life is better without you in it. It turns out that you put on a façade and lied to not only me, but my mom and sister as well. I don't like liars. For over ten years you kept some dark secrets and your true character hidden. I am grateful for the upbringing that I had because you were in the military as well as your service to our country. I loved you like my father and the person that you made yourself become. Was that a true person? I will never know. Why did I love that person? Was he even real? That I don't know. I don't regret loving the person who you morphed yourself into for however long. Though I question how real that person actually was.

      For several years you were as supportive a "father" as I ever had. I even called you daddy. During that time, you loved me for who I was. You supported every decision that I made and were there for me when I needed to talk to someone or a shoulder to cry on. As I got older I saw less and less of this. After your last deployment you completely changed. Is it war that changed you? Maybe, but some of the changes seemed calculated and almost too smooth. You slowly started picking fights with my mom over money thinking that I couldn't hear you. You were wrong, I could hear every freaking word and every word you spoke made me loose respect for you.

      You called us pigs or slobs every day. You stated that certain things would happen almost as if you planned them. Did you plan them? I will never know, but I do know that nine times out of ten they did happen. By the time my freshman year came to a close and we moved again. I noticed even more change. You became distant and fixated on going back to the Midwest, constantly saying that you regretted moving to Washington. You tried to convince me that I was from Michigan even though I barely have any memories there.

      Before my sophomore year you told me that with this school transfer you bet that I would drop out, calling me immature on a daily basis. You bullied me just as bad as the idiots at school. When I did decide to become homeschooled you called me a dropout claiming that I would never finish high school then saying that you would be my teacher, ultimately leaving me in the dust shortly after. You yelled at me for doing schoolwork and called me a failure. You put me in corners while you yelled at me like some sort of a crazed lunatic. You cooked with dairy and gave me daily stomach aches, claiming that I wasn't allergic to anything. You treated me and my family like garbage.

      Sound familiar? Well it should. You were like Aunt Brie round two for a few years. The day that my mom kicked you out was the best day of my life. In the moment I failed to realize one thing. The reason that I clung to you was because all I knew aside from mom was abuse. I desired the abuse because I didn't know any different. I wanted to fix you and make you the person that you falsely made yourself. Upon realizing that I knew I needed help to overcome it. I needed to make sure that I didn't get involved with an abuser in a future relationship. It was hard, but I have learned what a good friend is like. You are not it.

      When you did come back into our lives I immediately sensed a great sense of entitlement. Though you apologized, I wondered how sincere it was. You came back and acted like nothing ever happened after you totally left us in the dust. Thinking that we would call you daddy again or ever will. You have come out to visit a few times since that day. However, there is always a sense that you feel like you are in control when you are here. When you are where you belong, away from us.

Though you claim you want things to get better between all of us. You rarely call me, sometimes its weeks before I hear from you. For my mom you maybe call every few days.

On the days that you call you call multiple times almost like you are trying to make up for something. What are you trying to make up for? The insults and hatred that you spew at my mom? If that's the case, you are doing a pretty poor job at it. You basically left my mom alone with very little income to fend for ourselves. You do now support us financially when we need it. I guess that's a step, but what's the money worth without the effort to try to reconcile? Absolutely nothing! Yes, I do often have harsh words for you on the off occasion that we talk. What's wrong with me not taking abuse? Absolutely nothing, I shouldn't take abuse from anyone. Despite what you may think in your little nonexistent fantasy world.

When you talk to mom while I am around, you spew so much hate towards both of us. It's absolutely disgusting. You told me to get a job and that my book won't make it. All after you told me that my priorities are askew because you thought school wasn't my main priority and how lazy I supposedly am. You were sadly mistaken. My priorities are perfectly straight. School is a main focus of mine, but I also need a life. With the life that I have I don't have time to work full time. What "man" treats his wife and kids this way? Not any man that I know of.

Thank God that there are other men in my life to set an example for me. No mom is not dating them. They are just father type figures who came into the lives of Marissa and me when you decided to leave us in the dust. They set us straight when we are wrong, support every decision we make, encourage us, love us unconditionally and most importantly treat mom with full respect. They are true men who I am eternally grateful that they exist. They are our heroes who stepped up without thinking twice. You often make sick jokes about them which makes me loose even more respect for you. Not like I have any for you anyways.

    The day that you told me to kill myself when mom kicked you out is a day that I will never forget. You forced me to grieve the losses of two fathers. One that was a real man and then you who I thought was real, but I guess not. After you left I went through the grieving process of losing papa once again. Since you were around when he passed which I am grateful for. I was never really able to properly grieve his passing. I tried to hide it and push his family away. When I finally did grieve his passing properly I was no longer ashamed of growing up without him. I finally owned it and wasn't afraid what people thought should I make the choice to tell them about it.

    Instead of hiding who he was, I began to want to know more about him. I reached out to those who knew him. Unsure of how they would respond. I wasn't sure if I would end up reaching out to a closed door or an open heart. I got responses pretty quickly and for the first time in a while no longer craved abuse. I allowed myself to enjoy the different things that he did. I was proud of who he was and where I came from.

    If it seems like my life is better now. Your right it is. I no longer have to constantly deal with a liar. I have people who really love me unconditionally and don't lie about their pasts. I am on the way to finishing high school on time. I will be a success story no matter how stupid you think homeschooling is. Despite losing my real dad, I am a success story. Does this hurt to read? I'm sure it does. Think about how I felt when it happened. If you ever want to be friends again, you need to grow up first and learn how to become sincere. Then if that happens come talk to me. Adios

    -Alana

I am not Missing Out

As I prepare to enter my third and likely final year of homeschooling. Almost everyone tells me that I am "missing out" or "don't know what I am missing". The truth is that I know what life in a traditional classroom is like. I went to public school from kindergarten through 10th grade and it's just not for me. Hence I don't feel as if I am "missing out" on anything. I chose to leave public school in my sophomore year after going on five full years of bullying. The bullying lead to my grades slipping severely because I just couldn't focus. School was no longer a safe place. It seemed like a prison. Every day I went to class, I feared what was ahead. I enjoyed seeing the few friends that I did have, but knew that if I wanted a promising future, sacrificing that was something I had to do.

Since I made that choice two years ago I feel as if I am learning better than I ever did in a classroom. However, others including some family and friends don't seem to see eye to eye with me as far as that goes. Over the past three years I have heard statements or been asked questions that seem rather offensive. That have questioned the integrity or ability of those who is educating me. Some of those include. "How can a parent educate their child and expect them to thrive?" "You (or homeschooled kids in general) are way too sheltered." "I didn't know that your mom and or dad was such a _____(biologist, chemist, mathematician or what have you) that he/she could accurately teach you that." They have gone as far as to ask "Do you have any friends?" Unfortunately, many of those are direct quotes from family and friend or even total strangers.

Sometimes it feels like the bullying from family and friends is worse than it was in public school from my peers. To me it's amazing that people chose to bully someone over how they chose to get an education. Don't get me wrong, I am not anti-public school in any way whatsoever. I fully support public schools and think that they are great. I do however acknowledge that all kids learn differently and weather they are in a homeschool or public school environment those differences should be acknowledged. For me homeschooling is a better fit simply because of the freedom it offers me to explore. I have never been the most conventional person so I typically need a learning environment that is flexible.

    The style of homeschooling that we have chosen is a combination of styles. We call it traditional unschooling which basically means that I have books, but the end goal instead of doing a structured curriculum to get into college with a homeschool diploma is to take the GED as a way to finish high school. I do study, just like everyone else, but by the time junior year came around I have been able to set my own pace. I also use my surroundings to learn. The flexibility has allowed me time to do other things that I enjoy and want to pursue such as have a part time job and work on writing.

    I am homeschooled and don't feel as if I am missing out on anything. I have friends, go to social events, play mainstream high school sports and want to pursue a career. I am just life every other high school senior. I am different in how I chose to finish my high school education. What's so wrong with being different? We all deserve respect and acceptance. I am no exception. I also have a place in this world just like you do. Everyone is unique. You be you and let me be me. All I ask is that you be excepting of me just as I am of you. Differences are what make us all special.

Unheard No Longer

I am a survivor of child abuse. I will not say the name(s) of my abuser(s) however I will say this. It was not caused or encouraged by my parents or stepdad it happened years ago and has been addressed by the authorities. Child abuse seems to be such a taboo subject or just straight up ignored in this country. When the reality is that many of us have experienced it in some way or another. It shouldn't be taboo or ignored because if people keep ignoring the truth then many kids will feel worthless, like they deserve it or there is no way to stop it just like I did at some point or another. My abuser(s) tried to break me, but they didn't. I am the bigger, stronger person and my voice will no longer go unheard. It's my time to speak out. I choose now to begin to carry out the message that my dad wished to but it was too late for him to be able to do so. He passed away only a few months after sharing that message with me. Now is the time for me to carry out the message that he couldn't and stand up to end child abuse.

It Takes a Man to Be a Father

To the men who stepped up to help my mom raise us.

    Thank you for being a part of all of our lives. You picked up where papa left off. You didn't allow my past to define my future. You taught me what a true man should be like. You are the definition of the saying that it takes a village to raise a child.

    Thank you for selflessly stepping up and taking on that role of a father figure in our lives. Though many of you have your own children, you still show us unconditional love. You celebrate our victories alongside us. And aid us in overcoming our failures. You play the role of dad, even though you don't have to.

    You bring joy to our eyes. No matter how nearby or far away you may be. You teach us lessons about life that only a father can. You ease the emotional burden of being a single parent off of my mom by always being there. She can rest easy knowing that others love us as much as she does.

    You allowed me to once again trust men something that took me years to learn to do. You set an example for Marissa and me to follow. You preach the importance of taking the right path. You remind us of the legacy that the man who created us left behind. You praise us for doing something well. And reprimand us when we falter.

    I believe that God and our dad above put you all in our paths for a reason. You were meant to do the small things in our lives. The seemingly normal events that so many people take for granted. You will be the ones to question our first boyfriends. Hopefully not scaring them off too much. You along with my mom will be the one who he asks for my hand in marriage when the time comes. You along with my mom will one day walk me down the aisle and in papa's honor hand my heart to that man.

I can count on you for anything. I don't have to be afraid to be honest. I trust you as much as I trust my mom. You often share stories about mistakes that you have made in the past so I have something to learn from. Though you are far from perfect your wisdom is boundless.

You sometimes make me forget that my dad is indeed gone. You didn't take his place, but you did pick up where he left off so many years ago. You gave me back the part of my childhood that I didn't know I had lost. You replaced the feeling of innocence that I lost when he passed.

You praise me just like papa did. Those of you who knew him bring him up often. You tell me the kind of man he was. And answer the questions I have about him the best you can. You remind me that he is proud of me. Something that I am sometimes unsure of. You often make me laugh or embarrass me, just for fun.

You make sure that I don't miss out on anything that a dad would do. All of you make it impossible for me to say that I don't have a dad because I have so many men that love me. You may not have created us, but you love us as if you did.

Being a father to someone doesn't necessarily mean that you created them. Father is a title that is earned, not given. You all are family, even if our blood says otherwise. You will take us through life with a string head on our shoulders. You will set an example. You will remind us of papa. You will always love us like your own. And make good on your promises.

Thank you all for being real men. For always protecting us from evil. Thank you for doing the little things. Not one kind gesture goes unnoticed. Every phone call, text message and hug is appreciated. My life is a success because you all are a part of it. Thank you all for being a father to Marissa and I. A friend to my mom. And someone who loves all of us. <3Alana

Hey Papa Happy 50th!

Hey Papa Happy 50th! You are now officially getting really old. Although I was privileged to have over ten years with you here on earth and now over 7 and counting with you watching over me from heaven. I was too young at the time that you passed to understand your relationships with people outside of our immediate family. I also wanted to see whose lives you impacted in the 42 years that you were here on earth. So for your 50th birthday I decided to try to find out. I went on Facebook and asked everyone who knew you growing up or of you to tell me what kind of person you were. I usually don't ask for outside opinions or added content from anyone but mom but I figured that if I was going to find out who you were I may as well share it with the world. After all, this book is dedicated to you and sharing your message of forgiveness, humility and grace, as well as your sense of determination and pride with everything that you set out to accomplish. I was surprised with some of the responses.

"He was a class act and a great soccer player. Also a best friend to one of my best friends. O☺ <3"-Richard Kangas. One thing that you often talked about were your soccer playing days. I remember you saying that you were the goal keeper with the bright red hat. Seemingly the outcast of the team but that never stopped you from doing what you did best. Grandma used to always reminisce about your soccer days when she would ring the cow bell on the sidelines of your games growing up. Your soccer jacket also speaks for itself with all of the patches from the different tournaments that you played at. Your love for mom is evident even to this day. I often see the way that your friends treat her is what I remember the two of you being like during the time that you two were married and during the last year of your life (minus the romantic aspect). From what they all tell me I can only imagine the love and adoration that you two had for each other and hope that one day I will have friends like yours who feel the same about my future spouse.

"Jim was a great guy. That smile could light up a room. Wonderful guy and (a) good friend. XOXOXOXO"- Sandi McLane Bullington. Your smile is the one physical feature of yours that I distinctly remember. Hearing that others also feel the same way makes me understand that you were both an amazing father and a committed friend. It seems as though your presence in a room was always firm with some of the stories of your younger days that you told me when I was younger. I almost assumed that you were cocky and borderline arrogant in your high school days and younger years if I am totally honest (which I'm sure that you were at times). Hearing from your old friends has proven that mostly incorrect. Your smile will always be something I remember and hold dear to my heart, as will be your presence in a room. By the way Marissa has now become your clone. As I was looking through your cigar box with the old pictures in it, I found a picture with you holding a soccer trophy and had it not looked old I would have mistaken it for being her.

Two simple words "So young"- Debbie Sexton said about you describe your playful side to the tee. It often seemed like you were a teenager trapped in the body of a grown man. You were such a free spirit. There never seemed to be a set routine and almost everything but work was done on the fly. At work you were almost too serious (unless we went to work with you while you were in California) than as soon as you got home you were back to practically being a teenager again. You always wanted to be the fun parent like most dads. Mom was usually the disciplinarian when we were with her unless it was something major. If we really messed up, you would play the guilt trip on us a parenting classic that I now wouldn't fall for now but back when we were little worked like a charm.

"Jim was one of my oldest and best friends. He was funny, with that special sarcastic wit that made us all laugh. I miss him every day and know how proud he would be of you."- Chris Carney. To hear this from one of your best friends makes my world 100x brighter. I'm sure the added brightness has been put into my path as your sign that you are proud of what I am doing with my life. Your humor often consisted of making jokes about taking risks. Doing things where the outcome is never guaranteed. As a youngster I looked it as nothing more than childish humor, however looking back I realize that your jokes often had lessons hidden in them. With your sarcastic wit as it was so described, you weren't often one to sit down and have a serious conversation. Typically, you much preferred to make a joke about life instead of taking all of life too seriously. Even throughout your challenges, the one thing that you always took seriously was your family and friends. You were a committed friend to all of those who you cared about and never took anyone giving you trust lightly. Something that I still carry with me to this day.

"I didn't know him but I'll bet "Proud" fits very nicely."- Jim Connon. Often times I wonder if the path I have chosen to take has actually made you proud. It isn't one that many choose to take willingly. It's a path filled with times of uncertainty with hopes to one day make a lasting impact on this world. Drawing inspiration from those who have come before us, even then there is no one way to do things in this world that I have put myself into. After all I am one of the youngest to ever set out as someone to write a memoir. Actually often times when I tell people that I am writing a book at 17 they ask me what type of book I am writing and I tell them it's a memoir they either think I am joking or think I haven't lived enough to have a good story. That usually changes as soon as I briefly explain one, maybe two of the events that led me to begin writing this and tell them how you passed away. Then total strangers almost always tell me that you would be proud of the person that I have become, having never met you or me before. Even the doubters give me the strength and motivation that I need to move on. Usually those who place the greatest amounts of doubt on me or try to convince me to be more mainstream are the ones with the biggest secrets to hide. After all, "The very first step in healing is shattering the silence."- Erin Merryn

"Use to have Fun no matter what (.) Started from about Age 6 and I'm willing to BET it was Fun to the END!!! Was so many years ago just riding bikes and playing soccer all day everyday…."- Robert Mannino. I'm sure you and your little gang of friends had many fond memories growing up, I can only wish that you were here to tell us about them. As Marissa and I are getting older we are getting to the age where we are now able to reminisce about our younger years. We often wish that you were here to join the conversation. Growing up our childhoods were vastly different, yet strangely similar in some ways. Both Marissa and me have already moved state to state three times. First from Michigan to Washington when we were five and seven, then from Washington to Arizona when Marissa had just turned eight and I was three months before I turned ten and finally from Arizona back to Washington when Marissa was 13 and I was only a few days away from turning 15. Whereas you lived in one house for most of your childhood and part of your adulthood. Even then some of our fondest memories of growing up are of playing soccer and riding bikes with our friends in the various places we lived. Just like yours were. We definitely inherited your and mom's readiness to experience new things and have a good time. Probably doing it in a more refined way then you would have but still, ready to have fun.

"I went to school with him and had the pleasure of working with him. (He) Always made me laugh."- Leslie Larson RN. Like I said before you were known for your sense of humor.

The way that you would joke about kicking soccer balls at your parents' garage door which lead to it needing to be replaced three times or your little "pranks" on other people is what you were known for. I don't remember one family event or gathering where someone wasn't laughing at something you said or did weather it was appropriate or not. I also remember when you said something too out there or inappropriate grandma would at the top of her lungs yell "Anthony, what the heck do you think you are doing?!" That was usually followed by her joking about getting out the whiffle bat or broom to get you back in line if you didn't stop. She and mom were two of maybe three or four people who could put you back in your place that I knew of who you would listen to upon the first request.

"Loved Jim he was a great friend always up for a new adventure with a smile on (his) face. Going to his house was great there was always loud conversations with Grace will never forget …."-Scott Kwierant. Your sense of adventure was infectious to everyone around you. You put people at ease on those adventures with your presence. At our gatherings I have vivid memories of playing board games getting way too competitive at times. The volume of conversations was always loud, but those conversations were filled with laughter and memories. Sometimes it seemed like there were so many people around that it was a miracle that we knew all of them and fit them all into one house. The family members and friends blended together seamlessly into one amazing unit. When the cousins got together there was usually pranks being played or some sort of mischief on our end. We all seemed like siblings with the love for each other of a sibling. Although I was young when we moved to Washington and so was Marissa those are still some of our fondest memories to this day and forever will be.

"Happy 50th Birthday Uncle Jim. We only knew each other for a little while but within that little amount of time we made some awesome and fun memories on vacation and just around the house. You also allowed me to have two more cousins because if it wasn't for them I would only have two. I hope you have fun in heaven doing doughnuts in your little red sand car!" -Taylor Paulson. During the time we spent in California Taylor was like a big sister to Marissa and me. We practically did everything together with you. You always took us on amazing adventures, sometimes (more often towards the end of your life) mom was also there. The places that you took us always encouraged us to learn and use our imaginations to the fullest extent possible. You taught us the value of hard work and what a real man should be like. You weren't perfect, but that is why we all loved you so much because you weren't afraid to admit your faults. Even though you have been gone for a while the bond between the three of us is still strong and we still continue to learn from the lessons you taught us all.

Happy 50th Birthday Papa! I know that if you were still here there would be one heck of a celebration going on. Seeing the messages from everyone solidifies that you made an impact on this world in the 42 years that you were here on earth. So many people continue to love you and carry on your legacy and your fear of being forgotten is something that won't happen. We all love you so much and I can only hope that I am doing you proud by carrying out your message and legacy in the way that I am. Since your passing I have learned to accept mentorship from others that aren't blood, most of the mentorship I have received in life has come from your old friends. They have been the humblest and kindest people to step into my life. Many of them I hadn't talked to or met until after you passed but that didn't stop them from stepping up. Your girls are happy and taken care of. That doesn't mean that there haven't been challenges but we continue to move ahead. I hope you celebrated your 50th with a bang in heaven like you would have on earth. We all love you so much and know that you are watching over us from above. You were an amazing father, husband, son, uncle, brother, friend and family member to all and continue to be from up above.

Happy 50th!!!!!

Love all of us who continue to love and remember you here on earth!

"Basics build every complex system. They are the foundation. If the foundation is weak, the building will fall." -Mike Barwis

My name is Alana Gorski, the author of "The Newfound Legacy". Becoming a published author has always been something that I have dreamt of doing one day, but I never imagined that I would begin my journey at only 17. As you read through the collection of short stories leading up to this, my hope is that you tried to put yourself in my shoes and feel the emotion tied with each and every one of the stories. I have faced many challenges in my young life so far. Some say enough for two lifetimes. However, I believe that I am here for a reason, that reason is to impact the lives of many others. Even though my life for the past several years (from about age 5 on) has been a challenge, it didn't start off that way. My hope is that you use this as a guide to put the short stories together and make sense of everything that you just read.

My life started off pretty typical. I was born on June 4, 1998 to two happily married parents in just outside of Detroit Michigan. My dad aka papa was a hard working business man with an established career. My mom, a stay at home mom who had a 10+ year career as an accountant. Other than the fact that my parents were slightly older then the norm at the time I was born at 32 and 33 my life was relatively normal. My dad's extended family lived nearby, all but one of his sisters. Whereas my mom's was and still is scattered throughout the west coast and Midwestern parts of the U.S. We frequently got together with papa's family and extended family. The family gatherings were large and loud but always fun.

On March 10, 2000 my little sister Marissa was born and we became a family of four. At that point life was still pretty typical, however my dad started to have unexplained mood swings. Relatively infrequent at that time, but still very noticeable. He would go into almost this daze and go absolutely ballistic for a few minutes or a matter of 20-30 seconds. Immediately following the episodes, he would almost always wonder what was wrong with himself. That lead my mom to begin to believe that there indeed was something physical wrong with him. For the next three or so years the episodes became more frequent and intense to the point of her being forced to divorce him. The decision was made by the courts because they were so frequent that they were becoming potentially dangerous. Despite my mom's hardest pleas, they deemed him dangerous never bothering to do a CAT scan and investigate farther.

In 2003 the divorce became final and my mom was left a single mom with two kids struggling to get by. Even though I have no memory of this my mom said that at one point we were technically homeless living in a hotel. Throughout 2003 we had to move several times to basically hide from him because the court deemed him dangerous. If I remember correctly I went to three different schools in my kindergarten year. In March of 2004 when we were basically as settled as we could get in the home that we would only live in for about a year. My mom got a call from an old friend that she went to high school with. Paco was calling from Asia where he was stationed with the military asking if her and my papa wanted to hang out when he came to the states for a visit.

On the initial phone call that lasted several hours, she explained to her friend Paco that her and my dad were getting divorced and that he was no longer in the picture. She also told him that he was welcome to come and meet my sister and me, just for a visit. He gladly accepted and over the next few weeks they planned for him to come in and visit right after my sister turned 4 in March. During the first visit he quickly became more of a father figure in the lives of Marissa and I than anything. He also brought us back Korean money and handmade pajamas in backpacks that we thought were really cool at the time. Apparently the first time that he took me shopping I told someone that he was my new dad and we had just adopted him. His visit was brief, maybe about a week before he had to return to Asia to finish his one-year tour of duty. After his tour was over he was set to move to Washington state where he would be stationed for the next 4 years.

At first they were just planning on being friends and nothing more. Though they planned on just being friends it quickly became apparent that there was more than a friendship between the two of them. After the first visit they decided to follow the way things were going and enter a relationship. Both were newly divorced, but ready to begin their new lives together. Everything went from utter chaos and fear on our end to having some sense of normalcy once again. I remember after the first visit secretly hoping that they would one day get married. Paco seemed like everything that we needed and wanted in a dad. Everything that we didn't have at the time with our biological dad. Even before the relationship between the two of them became official without hesitation he stepped up as the dad in our lives and didn't look back.

By June of 2004 my mom and Paco decided that they wanted to get married. Three months later Marissa and me officially became military brats when they got married on September 11, 2004. They got married at a courthouse in Western Washington because at the time it was all that they had time to do. Our dad wouldn't allow us out of the state at the time so we stayed with him at his parents' house for the weekend while they got married. We were so excited to have a new dad, but at the time our papa's family all but accepted Paco. They scrutinized just about everything that he said and did. Often calling him names or saying that he was a flake out. Even though they knew that he was the one supporting us and being the dad that papa wasn't at the time.

It took almost a full year before my mom and stepdad convinced papa to allow us to leave the state and go to Washington for more than a weekend or week-long visit. By late August of 2005 they had finally convinced papa to allow us to move to Washington on the stipulation that he didn't have to pay child support something that made no difference to my mom and stepdad who by that point had fully become dad to us. That being said we were both giddy with excitement because we would soon be able to be a "normal family" as we told everyone. All we wanted was a mom and a dad living in one house. It never mattered to us weather Paco was blood or not, he was dad if he loved and took care of us.

From the point of papa agreeing to let us move to actually moving was a period of a few weeks, maybe a month at most. In that short amount of time my mom had to reenroll my sister and me in a school she hadn't seen across the country, decide what we would take with us (about a suitcase each) and what we would put in storage. She also had to get all of our medical records and the cat's who would be going with us and allow us to say goodbye to everything we had ever known. Looking back, I am dumbfounded as to how they managed to throw everything together in such a short period of time. Especially with the demands of papa and his family for more time to visit with us before we moved.

Moving day came on September 5, 2005 a beautiful early fall day that I remember all too vividly. It began before the sun even broke over the horizon. We awoke early in the morning, even before the sun broke the horizon. We gathered the last of our possessions that we could take with us including our cat Sweet Pea and prepared to leave. When it was time to leave we shut the door behind us preparing to meet my mom's good friend who would be taking us to the airport. As soon as the door was shut I remember a profound moment of stillness.

Almost as if to prepare us to accept the road ahead. The ride to the airport was a rather quiet one. Marissa, Sweet Pea and I were in the backseat. Very few words were spoken between Marissa and I other than usual childish excitement. We also said goodbye to papa and his family on the way.

Upon arriving at the airport after saying our farewells to the friend who took us to the airport and thanking him for the ride it seemed as if a beast was unleashed. Both Marissa and my energy levels went through the roof instantly. The chaos was unleashed. We quickly checked our bags and headed to security. Marissa and I were all for running around without shoes on like wild clowns. My mom wanted to run the other way. Probably because when we arrived at the security checkpoint they had some interesting instructions for my mom. She would have to remove Sweet Pea (a cat that didn't like to be held) from her carrier. Carry her through the metal detector with no leash or harness on. Then hold her so they both could be patted down and the carrier searched. My mom's face showed the sheer terror she must have felt in that moment. Thankfully her death grip on the cat didn't loosen and she was safely returned to her carrier without incident.

No sooner had we gotten through TSA did Marissa and I decide to almost start jumping off of walls. We were wild, probably due to lack of sleep, but who knows. My mom was tired, but had successfully navigated one airport. She only had one to go and could make it through anything by that point. Before we knew it the time came to board the plane. I remember wanting to enjoy the flight but finding it hard to be in the moment with the amount of excitement that I was feeling. Another highly profound memory that I have from that day is after boarding when the engines of the plane kicked on. Feeling the immense amount of power behind them was fascinating to me. Soon after the engines kicked on the sound intensified as we started to move faster and faster down the runway. Then we were off, headed to our new life as official military brats.

Once we arrived in Washington, life was back to normal. The only major adjustment that I remember being somewhat difficult was the time zone change. For the first few days it was hard internally being three hours ahead since Michigan is on Eastern Standard time which is three hours ahead of Pacific Standard time. After that hurdle was overcome it was smooth sailing. While we were in Washington we made new friends. The idea of living on a military base where other kids were like us with a parent or both who served our country was new to us. It was new, but a welcome concept. We soon became accustomed to hearing revile at 7AM and the National Anthem at 5PM to signal the beginning and end of the work day. Seeing others like Paco wearing uniforms, the occasional base wide lockdown and hearing the noises of jet engines at all hours of the day and night. It became so routine it was almost as if our old life in Michigan had never existed.

There were however subtle reminders in our day to day life such as phone calls to papa whom we thought was still in Michigan and a looming visit to Michigan. Little did we know he was not where he claimed he was and this would be our last visit at Thanksgiving for a very long time. As the weeks passed and the visit got closer we found out that to go to Michigan. We would be missing a few days of school prior to Thanksgiving break. We thought that was great. When the day came to leave for Michigan I remember being slightly nervous for what would be ahead but being ready for whatever came our way... Or so I thought. Everything felt routine the day we left, we got dropped off at the airport, went through TSA and waited to board the plane in Seattle. We made a call to papa who was anxiously awaiting our arrival in Detroit and took off for Michigan. Once we landed mom took us to the point at the airport where papa would be waiting for us at arrivals. After she dropped us off she would be heading back to Seattle until it was time for us to go home a week later.

As soon as we saw papa standing at the curb before we even said hello, it was evident that there was something different about him. His usual appearance was a slender six foot one-inch man with pale looking skin. The man that we saw looked just like him with a sun tan and some bulkier muscle on him. Other than that and the fact that he was driving his mom's minivan instead of his usual four-door sedan type car. Nothing seemed too out of the ordinary. As soon as we arrived at the house he shared with his parents. We were greeted by our cousins Kody and Katelynn that lived in Michigan as well as our Aunt Portia and Uncle Rodger. Aunt Portia and Uncle Rodger greeted us just as they had in previous years however our cousins both seemed on the shy side for the first little while. For the younger of the two, Katelynn the shyness wasn't out of the ordinary as she has always been more on the quiet side. However, for the older one Kody the shyness was highly unusual. Kody was more on the boisterous and arrogant side at times. He wasn't one to keep his opinions to himself.

After the initial greetings and the shyness had worn off the four of us were back to wreaking havoc on the world acting like siblings once again. Before we knew it the day before Thanksgiving had arrived and we began the process of soaking the turkey, breaking bread for stuffing and cleaning the house in preparation for the guests the next day. Something we had done every year prior. Only this year would be our last with everyone together as a family.

Thanksgiving Day seemed as it had every year prior. Family and friends came over to my grandmother's house to spend the day watching football, playing games and enjoying the company of one another. That year we followed tradition making the journey half way across the country from Seattle instead of from across town. There was a noticeable shift in how some of the family members and friends began to treat Marissa and I like outsiders in some ways. To me at the age of seven it felt like while we lived there we were a part of the family unit and when we came back after we moved they had broken away from that unit and made a new one. Despite feeling like we were being treated like outsiders we still enjoyed the rest of the day and Friday.

    Saturday is when everything changed and got even more confusing. That morning papa pulled a medium sized black rolling suitcase out of the closet in his room and began to pack. When we asked him why he was packing and where he was going he stated simply that he was packing to catch a flight "home." Initially he didn't elaborate any more than that until we refused to give up asking him where he had moved to because we thought he was still living in Michigan. Obviously that was no longer true. When he did eventually elaborate he said that he was catching a flight "home to California" where he now supposedly lived with a sister of his, Our Aunt Brie whom we barely knew. He claimed that he moved so he could be "closer" to us and wanted it to be a surprise.

    A surprise it was, but how welcome that surprise was, I am not quite sure. Upon moving to Washington our relationship with him had just begun to improve with the amount of telephone communication we had versus in person visits. Now that he had once again broken our trust and moved to the west coast without telling us. Not only that, but he was now also living with someone that we barely knew which was confusing to me. I didn't know whether to trust him just as much as I currently did or fear him more. I remember naively thinking that we were the only ones who didn't know about his last second departure. That theory was soon proven incorrect. We dropped papa off at the airport in the mid-afternoon on that Saturday. We would be spending one more full day and that night without papa in Michigan with our grandparents and cousins. We were scheduled to take the Sunday red eye from Detroit back west to Seattle.

We began to head to the airport just as the sun was about to set. The goodbyes to family and friends were pretty quick and before we knew it we were off. Upon arriving at the airport the sun was in the process of setting on an unusually clear day for that time of year. The sunset that day was a fiery orange and devilish red color. Upon arriving at the curb without papa in the car my mom's expression lead us to realize that we weren't the only ones who didn't know about papa's move west. The exchange between my mom and grandmother was fairly brief with very few words uttered between the two of them. In some ways the fiery colors in the sunset that day probably depicted the betrayal and rage that my mom must have been feeling, but was trying to hide. You could have cut the tension with a knife at that moment it was so intense.

After the exchange was over, the familiar chaos of being in an airport was unleashed. The next time we were set to visit papa was for about a week on Christmas break. That next visit would be our first to California to visit him. The flight back to Seattle was routine and uneventful. When we first called papa from the airport after we arrived, it was strange. He was now on the same time zone we were for the first time since we moved west. After one free day off of school since we returned late on a Sunday our life as military brats was back to normal. We enjoyed living on the base where my stepdad worked because of the routine, structure and pride that goes along with living that lifestyle. It was normalcy for once. The calm before the storm.

"As in so many cases of sexual abuse within the family, it is much more complicated than had it been done by a total stranger."- Erin Merryn

Christmas time came quickly and before we knew it we spent our first Christmas morning in Western Washington. We were to head off the next morning for our first trip to California. The drive from where we lived Western Washington to papa's new home was over 18 hours one way. Prior to the trip we were excited to see/meet all of the cousins that lived there. All but one, who a few years prior on one of her few visits to Michigan when I was maybe four or five locked one of my other cousins, my younger sister and me in a room telling all of us that my mom was a bitch. She was even evil enough at about age six or seven to convince my directly older cousin to say it once as well even though she didn't mean it. Her mom (my Aunt Brie) from past experiences seemed untrustworthy for a reason I had yet to identify. Being so young and having their visits be so brief I was unable to see past her exterior portrayal until we spent more time together.

	By the time we arrived in California for that first visit the sun had already set. My mom and papa had agreed to meet at a spot about 20 minutes or so from where he now lived. Once we arrived at the meeting spot and spotted papa's new giant pickup truck for the first time, it sunk in that we had arrived. After a 20 or so minute drive we finally arrived at papa's new house. The gate surrounding it looked like the gate to a dungeon in the dim light. He quickly punched in the code to the gate and hurried us inside to greet our cousins who were waiting inside. Upon arriving inside we were told that Santa had come to their house for us. We were also told that we now lived in California as well, which we knew wasn't true, by Aunt Brie. We had been weary of her from the beginning, she just seemed off.

	After we opened our presents it was time to head to bed which wasn't all that hard after the amount of travel we had just done. The first morning was confusingly busy. We were used to busy mornings, but in Washington the busier mornings were structured. Structure was something that I noticed instantly that this environment was lacking. During breakfast, which I remember to have been rather brief it was announced with great enthusiasm by everyone at the table that we would be having a pool party later that day. So before we could even get a grip on our new surroundings or the house really for that matter we were thrown into cleaning it for a party that we knew nothing about. For us having Christmas parties other than at school on holidays was strange. As soon as that was announced I remember going from feeling somewhat welcome by papa and two of the three cousins to feeling like a total outsider.

      After breakfast everyone went in different directions to clean whatever was necessary to prepare the house for the party. My Aunt Brie forcefully instructed me to begin to clean and dust. I hesitantly agreed to do it in fear that I would be punished. That time she didn't necessarily threaten punishment. However, her tense body language and blank stare suggested that she was hinting that way should I not comply. Papa and our Uncle Ben were around for the first little while of the cleaning process. That is until they decided that they had to leave to run errands and pick up our cousin Tiffany from her mom's house. Although Tiffany made an appearance the night before to open presents she returned to her mom's house for the night because she had other plans for the next morning.

      As soon as papa and Ben shut the door quite literally all hell broke loose. Aunt Brie and our older cousin Ava went from being harsh with tense body language to straight up crazy. They began to treat Marissa and I especially, like total slaves. They ordered me to mop, vacuum, wipe surfaces, dust and do the dishes in the tone that you would use to scold a dog. Ava and Aunt Brie threatened physical harm to me and my family should

I not submit to them and obey their orders. I felt helpless, but determined to do as I was told to avoid getting myself or my family hurt in any way. As I was frantically doing as I was told I vividly remember Ava being at my heels the entire time. She was telling me that I was a waste of valuable fucking space on this earth, a worthless little shit head, a stupid piece of scum, that my mom was a fucking bitch and reminding me of what would happen should I not comply.

The one time that I did not comply due to not knowing the location of the materials necessary for the task I feared that I would be punished and I was. Aunt Brie picked me up from where I was standing, ran me down the hall into a dark room which happened to be Ava's. She shut and locked the door and began the punishment. She first called me a mother fucking idiot as well as a worthless little shit among other things proceeding to hit me across the backside with some plastic object multiple times. After she was done beating me she pulled down my pants and stuck her finger up between my legs and into my vagina. She then explicitly told me that if I told anyone she would get an AK47 or a shotgun and use it to kill my mom in front of me also making it very clear that there would be more beatings to look forward to in the future. To finish it all off she forced me to when asked who my favorite aunt was, answer that she was. Should I note there was also a threat for severe punishment with that.

As soon as her little rampage was over as instructed I returned to cleaning and doing what I was told. When papa and Uncle Ben returned home with Tiffany, Aunt Brie did as all master manipulators do she made it seem like nothing happened. Papa and Uncle Ben quickly put away and set up everything that they had purchased for the party. By the time everything was set up there was some time before guests were set to arrive so papa and Uncle Ben asked us all if we would join them for a swim. We all agreed and I acted like I was excited when I was actually internally freaking out because of the bruise on my backside. I prayed to God that my swimsuit covered it because I knew that if it didn't and papa saw it all hell would once again break loose. I wanted to avoid that scenario at all cost.

As I was putting on my swimsuit I was beyond relieved that it indeed covered the bruise. I knew that for at least the next while I wouldn't be getting punished. Swimming numbed both the physical and emotional pain of what had just happened. While we were still in the pool the guests began to arrive. They all seemed nice, but very different to the crowd of people that we were used to being around. What also seemed strange is that some of them didn't bother to introduce themselves even when we asked. Not long after the guests finished arriving, the party began to feel out of place for the time of year. Almost like it should have taken place on the 4th of July instead of at Christmas time. Most of the adults were consuming massive amounts of alcohol and some were so drunk that they were acting like little kids. Although the seemingly out of place party was fun I could still see Aunt Brie's glares from across the room and pool. The hatred that she had for me was evident and I could do nothing about it. Nor did I desire to.

The next few days went pretty smoothly. I was able to finally get a true idea of my surroundings and get to know two of the three cousins (one older and one younger) better. Then came New Year's Eve when there was set to be yet another party. The routine from the last one repeated. We had a quick breakfast, started cleaning the house and the guys left to run errands. This time the abuse that ensued was emotional because Tiffany was at the house. So it was all pretty discreet and went unnoticed by the other kids. Ava and Aunt Brie would give me the look of doom as often and when possible make sure to remind me of a few thing, one that I was worthless and two that I was a fuck up were their choices that day. When papa and Uncle Ben got back the pattern repeated and we once again were ready for the party.

The New Year's Eve party was even more chaotic and unfamiliar than the one for Christmas. What made it seem even more like the 4th of July was the fact that they guys would be lighting off fireworks. Some of the guests who attended the Christmas party were also there, but most of the people were new. Most of the new guests were rather on the rude side. They treated us like outsiders and acted like we should have known all of their names instead of addressing them by sir and ma'am. Even then the party was enjoyable, but I remember longing for what I had in past years. When we would all gather at my grandparents' house, roast marshmallows in the fireplace and drink hot chocolate while trying to stay awake long enough to watch the ball drop at midnight. Then heading home to begin the new year or spending the night at my grandparents' house before heading home in the morning.

A day of two after our one last hoorah we were headed back to Washington. I was so relieved because it was only after the New Year's party that I realized the gravity of the abuse that had just happened. I became terrified of everyone except Marissa, Tiffany who we had grown close with and looked to as a big sister and Willow our little cousin. I thought of every possible way to leave there early and considered calling the cops, running away or trying to sneak away with Tiffany who was headed back to her mom's house the same day we were leaving. She was leaving just an hour or two earlier so I felt like if necessary it would be a viable option. However, I felt that if I did any of those Aunt Brie would either harm me, kill my mom, prevent me from calling her when we came back or kidnap me.

Saying goodbye was a tragic relief. It was difficult to so long to Tiffany and Willow. I would call it neutral saying goodbye to both Uncle Ben and papa because they had not proven to be entirely trustworthy, but nothing shot off alarm bells with them. Saying goodbye to Aunt Brie and Ava felt amazing and eerie at the same time. They forced me to hug and say that I loved them which made me sick to my stomach. Aunt Brie also made sure to say that she hated me in my ear before releasing me from her devilish grips. The drive to meet my mom was relatively brief, but felt as though it took hours. Once we were with our mom and papa had left the terror set in. Only minutes into the 18-hour drive from Southern California to Western Washington I began to ask my mom if we were out of California yet.

She calmly assured me that we would be soon and asked me if I was alright. Though I said yes, my assurance to her was far from believable. She went on to continue driving and made sure to tell me when we were out of California. When we were finally in Oregon, which seemed to take forever I told her a few things, but was rather vague making sure to leave out what I was specifically instructed not to talk about. We arrived back in Washington early the next morning and went back to our normal routine. In early March of 2006 we moved and transferred schools once again. This time to a small island with a population of just 1,200 people about an hour away from the base that Paco worked on. The island was amazing, so serene in every way. We thought that it was especially cool to have to go over a bridge to get to our new school in the neighboring town. At our new school we quickly made friends and became adjusted to the slower pace of life on the island.

Our new house sat on slightly over an acre of land with plenty of room to run and play. The top level of the four-part yard was fenced with fruit trees, a grape arbor and a small patio. That transitioned into a large grassy area on a hill with a lavender and rosemary bush as well as wild blueberries and strawberries that on the rare occasion it snowed we could sled down. Behind the grassy area was a massive garden and wooded area that seemed to go on for miles. There weren't many neighbors super close by. So after school we often played with the other kids who lived on the island at the bus stop which was about a mile away at the fire station. That is when the weather was nice. Sometimes we would go home with one of the neighbors who used to drive his tractor sometimes to pick us up. That routine became so normal that it was unimaginable we could ever break it… Until our week long spring break came when we had to go back to California once again.

    When the time came to return to California for a second visit a mix of extreme fear of Aunt Brie and Ava ran through my body as well as mild excitement to see papa, Tiffany and Willow. I remember being so confused as to how I should feel before heading down to visit. So I just put it out of my mind and decided to just try to enjoy the long road trip ahead. That time if I remember correctly we left after the sun had set and arrived in California as it was rising. Along the way I vividly remember the Cascade Mountain Range in Oregon being lit by the silver moon and the fruit trees of Central California being kissed by the golden early morning sun. The 18-hour drive flew by and it was only after my mom left us with papa that the confusing wave of emotions washed across my body once again.

"I am prepared for the worst, but hope for the best." -Benjamin Disraeli

On the relatively short drive back to the house that papa lived in with his sister. We were told that we would be going on a week-long trip to the desert. While we were there we would be staying in Uncle Ben's RV, riding quads and dune buggies and doing camp fires every night. Since we now lived in such a small town going back to California was a huge shock. Aside from Seattle it was the busiest "city" that we had recently been to. Everything was once again close by and it seemed like you could pretty much walk anywhere. Upon arriving at the gate that even in the sunlight, it looked like a dungeon. I began to put up defensive walls to prepare myself for the abuse I feared would be coming.

As soon as we entered the gate, everyone came rushing out of the house. Most all of them seemed friendly and welcoming including Aunt Portia and Grandma Elizabeth who were also visiting at the time. All of them but Aunt Brie and Ava. The look in their eyes was the same emotionless hatred that I remembered seeing when she was molesting me as well as when Ava was at my heels degrading me. I remember being quiet despite all of their welcome excitement while Marissa who had just turned 6 at the time joined in. That was the very first time I was called the little tattletale and 20Q by several of them except papa, Marissa and Willow. Willow was giving me a huge hug telling me that she loved and missed me. They all asked me if I was being so quiet because I was a little tattletale. Truth is I hadn't told my mom all that much, Marissa had also confided in my mom. I was actually quiet out of fear, not guilt. It was after calling me a tattletale or bratty little tattletale, that the same people called Marissa the good little princess.

At that point even though I had only been there five minutes I had enough and part of me wanted to leave. Part of me also hoped that the vacation would be a reprieve from the chaos. We went inside where the noise level increased tenfold and everyone got busier packing for the trip to the dunes. Since we had just taken a trip to get there we were already packed so we decided to ask permission to go play in the living room with Willow. Papa said yes so off we went to just be kids. Little did we know Aunt Brie and Ava were lurking around the corner in the kitchen waiting for any opportunity to strike.

Strike they did, every time Marissa and Willow would go to a different part of the living room I was nailed with some kind of hatred. They threw a water bottle at me, knocked me in the back of the head claiming it was an accident on their way to grab the vacuum from a closet. They also called me horrendous names such as a fuck up, worthless little shit (a favorite of theirs), a bratty tattletale and a dumb asshole. Following that was the usual threat of beatings should I make a noise or tell anyone. I felt betrayed that papa would let this happen under his watch and not do anything. I felt that he basically should have had eyes everywhere. Looking back, I realize that he could have done nothing unless I told him which I was too afraid to do. Abusers like these idiots are sadly masters at their craft and how and when to abuse people usually thinking that they are above the law and will never get caught.

Later that day all of the kids and papa boarded the RV to spend the night because we were set to leave early the next morning. We did indeed leave early, around 5AM for the six-hour drive ahead. I remember waking up with the other kids around 7-8AM excited to be on the road and wanting to already be there. We played games and watched movies until we arrived around lunch time. By then we were all eager to get outside and run off some energy. That is after the guys safely unloaded all of the quads and dune buggies and set up camp while we ate lunch inside. It was a shock to us to see so much sand around. In every direction, all you could see was sand. We had only ever seen that much sand on a beach, this time there was no water. Just sand for miles and miles.

As soon as camp was set up we all had a safety meeting about the proper uses for helmets, gloves and goggles as well as how to safely turn everything on and off. After the safety meeting papa and Uncle Ben loaded all of us up in the dune buggies and headed for the dunes. We went so fast that it almost felt as though we were flying over the sand and not actually on it. The first time I saw the sand dunes from a distance I was captivated by how massive and steep they were. Upon arriving we stopped at an area next to the dunes that had a steep bowl looking area of sand near it. We instantly wanted to get out and play when we saw it. So play we did. We slid down the sides and raced to get back to the top. After what seemed like hours of fun we loaded back up in the dune buggies and got our first taste of riding the dunes.

Riding the dunes was an adrenaline rush that I had never felt before. It was terrifying and amazing. By the end of that experience I remember being beyond tired, but that wasn't the end of it. As soon as we were finished riding the dunes, we were off to the drag races. I had never seen so many dune buggies and quads in one place going so fast. The noise level seemed equivalent to standing next to the engine of a running jet. Except without ear plugs on, the only thing to dull the noise was our helmets. It was insane and before we knew it we were lined up next to another dune buggy ready to race. Once the race started I realized that I had never in my life gone so fast aside from being on a plane. Once the race was over the guys driving the buggies were betting a beer for each loss to drink after we got back to camp.

By the time the races were over for the day and we made the trek back to camp for dinner the sun was set. Papa and Uncle Ben immediately began to build the bonfire along with Tiffany's uncle Jason who also came along with us for the week. Once the fire was built and dinner was over while we roasted marshmallows the guys began to drink. Uncle Ben took it to the extreme and drank most if not all the beers he had won from the drag races which totaled 5-6 maybe 7. While papa only indulged in one or two, saving the rest for a later time. The next day I woke up with a rash on my backside so papa put cream on it in the morning and we went on with the rest of the day's activities. Then when it was time to reapply the cream Aunt Brie took it upon herself to offer to do it.

Inconceivable fear immediately rushed through my veins because I feared that she was after more than doing a favor for my dad. Even then I dared not to say anything fearing the repercussions if I did, so I went with it. By that point my trust in Aunt Brie was a level zero, so my fear was warranted. As I feared upon going inside she locked the door to the RV. She forcefully pulled down my pants and with cream on her finger made sure to fondle my genitals for what seemed like hours and stuck her finger up my vagina once again. While doing this she called me a bratty tattletale, a useless scumbag, telling me that my mom was a bitch and wh***e and calling my stepdad either a w**b**k or a s***k. Finishing her little rodeo with the same threats about not telling anyone that I became so used to hearing by that point.

As soon as it was over as I went outside and attempted to act normal. I tried block out the fear that was lurking in my mind. She also instructed me to once I was outside explain to everyone how amazing she was for being so kind as to help me feel better. I did as I was instructed to and moved on. It took me a while to forget the blank, hateful look on her face that she always had when she was abusing or molesting me. To this day it is one of the only features of hers that I vividly remember. The last four or five days of the trip were the same routine of papa putting cream on me and doing it respectfully. Then Aunt Brie doing it at night. Taking it too far every time without fail, following with the same litany of names and threats and when going outside upon being instructed to, telling everyone how amazing she was.

The times during the day and mornings of the trip were highly enjoyable and greatly treasured. We quickly became used to being outside all day every day. Just riding the quads and dune buggies and playing in the endless amounts of sand. At one point I fell off of my quad and it ran over me leaving me with burns on the backs of both of my calves. Aunt Brie wouldn't allow papa to properly treat them because she hated me so much. On the last night of the trip we all gathered to celebrate Marissa and papa's birthdays.

Although it was April by that time and they are both in March, the family decided to celebrate them while we were all together. That was the year that papa turned 40 when everyone thought he was "over the hill" and Marissa turned 6. We celebrated with a yellow cartoon cake that both of them had requested. I remember being happy about celebrating their birthdays and feeling accepted and loved by Marissa, papa, Willow, Aunt Portia and I guess you can say Tiffany. However, the rest of the family members and friends treated me like either a third wheel or nuisance. I remember feeling utterly confused, but just sticking near the small group of people who appreciated me and enjoying their company. It was on that trip that we also found out that Aunt Brie was pregnant with another baby.

The night after the birthday celebration it was time to drive overnight back to the house papa shared with Aunt Brie. Arriving back at that house I felt a massive rush of fear and relief. I was hoping that Aunt Brie would keep her act together for the rest of the day until we left. Even then I was constantly on alert like I always was. I was relieved that other than a few dirty, heartless looks and snide comments, she did. Saying our goodbyes to Willow was heart wrenching and nearly as difficult to Tiffany as we had all grown so close. Tiffany now felt like a big sister and Willow a little sister. The group of people who it was neither difficult or easy to say goodbye to had grown to Uncle Ben, Tiffany's uncle Jason, Aunt Portia, Grandma Elizabeth and papa. We didn't necessarily want to leave them quickly but no tears were shed in doing it. As usual saying adios to Aunt Brie and Ava was a relief. Although I remember telling both of them I loved them. It was only because I was instructed to by both of them. I didn't really mean it one bit.

After saying goodbye, it was time to go meet up with our mom. Only moments after reuniting with our mom, after papa left Marissa and I began to ask if we were out of California yet. Like she had the last time, she reassured us that we would be soon. Once we got into Oregon we confided in her a small amount making sure to leave out the details that Aunt Brie explicitly instructed us not to mention out. Once we were back in Washington we went back to our normal routine. It was like a switch would turn on and off between California and Washington. After this visit we would talk to papa on the phone more often than we had after previous visits. Now while we were talking to him we also often times talked to Willow. Who at the age of not even two would tell me that she loved and missed me every time. Tiffany would also sometimes talk to us which was exciting.

Often times when we would talk to papa he would be running after and taking care of Willow. He seemed to care more about her then either of her parents did and basically raised her. When she was around him she looked to him like he was her prince. Papa's bond with her was amazing. He even called her "Phyllis" after the world famous comedian Phyllis

Diller because of her wild morning hair. The Willow that I remember at that age was a wise beyond her years, high energy little spitfire. She always had something witty to say and constantly made everyone laugh. She was so smart that by the age of two she figured out how to steal papa's phone and call us or my mom without his knowledge until he caught her. She also called my mom her mom claiming that Aunt Brie wasn't her mom, she was a bitch. In fact, one of her favorite things to do from the time she was about two was to walk up to total strangers and explain to them that her mom Brie was a bitch. She also told me that a few times when we talked on the phone.

After we got back from our spring break trip one of the neighbors offered Marissa and me our first job as ranch hands. We would work a few hours a week for $20, a dozen eggs that we got to pick out and organic fertilizer for our garden. We gladly accepted and every week showed up on time and happily did our jobs on the days we were scheduled to. I remember loving being around the horses and chickens. Even though my job was to clean up after them, I still loved every second of it. Once we began our jobs our life seemed complete and it was. Grandma Mary, mom's mom even moved in with us which we thought was cool. She brought a cat friend named Zorbie with her. He and our cat Sweet Pea got along pretty well. Although he looked more like our black lab Princess, even drinking out of the toilet if we let him. We loved him like he was ours from the start and gladly welcomed him and Grandma Mary into our family.

Before we knew it school was out and it was time to head to California yet again. By this time my fears of going there had reached their peak. This time instead of going to visit for a week or two we were headed down there for over a month. The fear that we were going alone was almost paralyzing. Even then I packed up and went anyways. Still terrified of telling my mom much about what happened in fear of retaliation. The 18-hour drive from Washington to California was a rollercoaster ride of emotions. There was excitement, terror, fear and anticipation. Through all of those emotions there was a constant hesitancy about seeing Aunt Brie specifically. She was pregnant with another baby. So she was the only one of the clan that I thought would be unpredictable. I had already preconceived that Uncle Ben would probably get drunk, papa would be okay, Tiffany maybe call me a tattletale or 20Q, Willow would be happy, Ava would be cruel and that's about it. Aunt Brie had abused me in the past. Now that she was pregnant I was unsure if it would get better or worse.

We arrived at the same meeting spot as we had the past few visits and made the same eerily familiar drive from the meeting spot to the house. When we arrived at the gate, it still looked like a dungeon/prison to me. This time some people were outside to greet us, while others stayed inside. Those who were outside seemed to not care as much they were visibly excited, but seemed more interested in whatever else they had going on. When we went inside there were already people over to visit. Uncle Ben's side of the family seemed pretty welcoming. His mother whose name I will not mention treated us like her own grandkids. She was our savior when Aunt Brie or Uncle Ben acted stupid and we had to leave the house. We often stayed with her if that happened. As usual the gathering that day felt slightly out of our comfort zone (though quieter than usual) but it was reasonably enjoyable.

The summer of 2006 is a confusing blur of events. So much happened that I sometimes feel as though I am trying to put a puzzle together that will never fit. So much chaos ensued that it's hard to believe it could all happen within such a short period of time. We fell into a "routine" I guess you can call it that summer. Most of the week days were spent around the house with as irresponsible nanny that Aunt Brie hired who seemed to care less about us. The various nannies that the family went through usually seemed to know and care more about house cleaning then they did kids. There were many days when Tiffany or I was basically put in charge of Marissa and Willow. We basically had to learn how to take care of ourselves and for Tiffany and me, the other kids as well. Ava was sometimes around as well when she wasn't at acting camp or her dad's house. She was never anything more than a bully who tried to treat us like her personal servants.

On occasion if we didn't know how to do something, we were forced to ask Aunt Brie how to do it. She worked from home, but almost never came out of the office during the day. That is unless she got pissed off at something that Ava told her we supposedly did or she just felt like taking her fury out on us for no reason. Though Tiffany now refuses to believe that I was abused or call her own experiences abuse it was usually her or me that ended up getting the brunt of it. When we were both together Tiffany usually got it worse, but when she was with her mom I got it equally as bad. Sometimes something as simple as asking her how to change Willow's diaper that she refused to change would set her off. Sometimes she was pleasant and gave us a vague answer. Almost implying with the way that she looked at us that we should have already known how to do it. We usually kept ourselves occupied by doing our summer workbooks for school, going outside, riding quads (4 wheelers), playing with the horse or the dogs. Sometimes when Tiffany was around or Aunt Brie decided to come out of her lair (office) for a while, we would go for a swim.

Most of the days where I was basically left in charge at only eight were filled with some kind of abuse. Aunt Brie would do anything from lock us in rooms for hours to beat the snot out of us with spoons or whatever else she could find. She called us bratty little shit heads, fuck ups, even going as far as to call my stepdad a w*t b**k and a sp**k as well as my mom a wh**e and a bitch. Often times between phone calls or whatever Aunt Brie would order me to come into her office. Just to call me a name or tell me how awful I supposedly was. Following with her usual question of who was my favorite aunt. I had to reply that she was. The one time that I decided to stand up for myself and give my true answer I regretted instantly it because she spanked me so many times that I lost count some of them through my pants and some of them across my bare butt. Thankfully she didn't go any farther than spanking me across my bare butt after pulling my pants down. Still though it is inconceivable to me now how anyone could do that an innocent child.

On the very rare occasion that Ava was around when Tiffany wasn't. She was so vulgar that instead of Willow calling her A for Ava like she did T for Tiffany. She told everyone that A stood for asshole, which was pretty accurate in my opinion. Ava acted like she was the queen and we were her minions. Ava did everything that she could to get attention on herself. Everything from purposefully trying to drown herself in the pool to slamming her head on the side of the pool for whatever reason and even stealing papa's credit card once and trying to use it. The way that I would describe her is attention seeking con artist who likes to bully other people for the fun of it. On the days that we went swimming she would always force me to change with her. While we were in the room (usually her bedroom or the bathroom) she would force me to undress in front of her to prove I was a girl. Sometimes she would even make me lay on the bed or floor so she could see between my legs and my yet to develop breasts. Every single time the same stupid routine.

When papa and Uncle Ben were around, the abuse usually stopped. I emphasize the word usually because that wasn't always the case. Sometimes Aunt Brie or Ava would sneak it if I had a rash or something like that from a zinc deficiency that I was born with. If that was the case Aunt Brie almost couldn't resist the opportunity to sneak something. She would usually like before claim that she was going to put cream on my rash. Then take it a step farther and stick her finger up my vagina as far as it could go. Her new threat was that if I told anyone, not only would she kill my mom in front of me she would call the police and claim that I kicked her in the stomach and have me arrested. When she or Ava didn't choose to strike, the afternoons and evenings were spent swimming, playing outside with papa and watching TV or a movie. The nights were often late, but I basically lived for them because I could finally relax.

    Sometimes we were able to go to work with papa and or Uncle Ben. We loved going to work with them because we could spend time together with him without having to worry. Every morning that we went to work with papa, we stopped at the same gas station that he always did. He would buy us snacks for the day and sometimes other things. While we were at work with papa we ran wild at times. We loved meeting all of his co-workers who treated us like their own kids. Playing with the copier and staplers as well as other office supplies was something that I remember to be particularly exciting for whatever reason. As was running through the break room like a bunch of wild clowns.

    When he had to go check on a jobsite we always went with him. Sometimes the drive from work to the jobsite was long, but it was treasured. We almost hoped it would be long because papa would not be distracted for a longer period of time. We would have him to ourselves and his undivided attention on those car rides. We often talked about the little things. During those drives, I saw a glimpse of the father that I barely remembered trickle through the façade that he had put up. He was goofy and always joked about whatever came to mind. When we arrived if it was safe papa would show us around. We would learn the process of building the different things that they were working on and the tools necessary to complete the task. When it was time to head back we would usually stop somewhere for lunch and have even more time with him. Not sure how much work he actually got done on the days that we were with him. I did see a true father which is more important and meaningful than any job ever will be.

On weekends we would usually try to go to the beach or somewhere in the Los Angeles area. Huntington Beach was our favorite beach and city. We loved not only the beach and pier, but also the city itself. Papa always parked near the same spot and if it was early enough in the day, we would look at some of the shops next to the beach. Some of the shops sold hermit crabs that we always tried to convince papa to buy us. He always refused because he said that they die too easily. One time when Ava was with us, Aunt Brie got her one and it died about a month later. Point proven papa. We also loved playing in the water and sand all day trying not to get sun burned. The group that usually went was Willow, Tiffany, Marissa, me and papa. On occasion if the Seattle or Detroit team was playing, we would go to a baseball game in the area.

Unfortunately, the good times at times seemed hard to come by. Though we had fun on weekends or the rare occasion that papa took us to work. A majority of the time was spent at the house with Aunt Brie. That first summer I felt like I had grown up a decade. When I left Washington I was a normal eight-year-old. When I was set to return, I thought that my peers would ostracize me because of how much I thought that I had grown up. The exact date of our return to Washington was kept a secret from us because papa claimed that it would make us enjoy our time there less. It didn't help our anxiety a bit, but it was usually so chaotic that we were lucky if we even knew the day of the week. That summer I inadvertently learned what alcohol can do to someone because Uncle Ben always drank. He never stopped, often stating that you only live once.

When papa caught him doing it, he would either ask him to stop or if it was a weekend join in. Though at times he was irresponsible, papa never got drunk. As the summer went on it felt longer and longer. Midway through it I had put up so many walls that I was basically living in a box. Even Tiffany was a bully at times. She called me names such as freak, tattletale and party pooper. To be totally honest though I loved her like a sister. Despite what she thought, with the amount of walls I had up she barely knew me. In fact, that's probably true for most of them. Having lived through so much at such a young age I got so good at living behind walls that I could trick almost anyone.

If anyone asked me a question about anything but my life in Washington, I would often tell them a total lie. Something that I made up on the spot. I did this so I didn't have to get emotionally invested. So that I could protect myself in case their response was not a positive one. If I was asked something as simple as my favorite food or I would make something up. I feared that every interaction with anyone would somehow end up being something negative. The only time that I didn't have the walls put up all the way up was when it was just papa, Marissa, Willow and me. I also got so good at having them up and working around those barriers, that I could control when I put them up and when I worked around them. It wasn't something that I did to be deceitful it was my way of self-preservation. I knew that if I didn't have them up then everything would begin to get to me. They are what helped me get through the summer without going insane.

August came around and we knew that we would finally be going home within that month. I was so excited to finally see my mom again after so long. We had talked over the summer on the phone, but it wasn't the same as being with her in person. I remember trying to not let myself get too excited because Aunt Brie saw emotion as weakness. That was the time when I felt as though I had to put the walls up the highest. Though the abuse still ensued, I knew that if I allowed myself to be excited that it would get worse. So I just took whatever she threw at me, kept my mouth shut and went on.

In late August Grandma Elizabeth came out for a visit. During her visit I saw a side of her that I never wanted to know even existed. She fed into Aunt Brie's hateful comments abusing both Marissa and I physically and verbally. I was spanked several times and my sister was dragged down a carpet hallway. We were locked in rooms by both of them for hours on end if we were bad. Grandma Elizabeth also took it upon herself to take a picture of me and Willow in the shower. Totally naked and exposed, after I remember explicitly telling her no. Marissa being dragged was the last straw. We were done. So we somehow got to a phone and told my mom to come pick us up now. So pick us up she did. This time saying goodbye was the best day of the visit. I couldn't wait to get the heck out of there. As usual the only person that was difficult to say goodbye to was Willow. I would also miss Tiffany but not as much after her intermittent episodes of straight up petty bullying.

"Let's create, not destroy. Let's believe and not doubt." -Derek Hough

Seeing my mom was to that point the best day of my life. As soon as we got into the car, we began to ask her if we were out of California yet. She calmly reassured us that we would be soon. Once we finally were, which seemed like it was days later. We told her as much as we thought that we were able to without getting hurt. No more and no less. Then as soon as we got back home and unpacked it was back to getting ready for school for the 2006-2007 school year my third grade year. By that time, I was so excited about finding out who my teacher was and what friends of mine were in my class. It was as though I almost didn't care what happened over the past summer. Life went on. The only constant subtle reminder of the events the previous summer was talking to papa on the phone.

Once school started I knew that I was back where I belonged. I made amazing friends and had a teacher that I will never forget. My teacher that year fostered such a rich and fulfilling learning environment and was incredibly encouraging. After a pretty ordinary start to the school year, November rolled around. It was time to once again visit papa in California. This visit was set to be pretty short which, was a relief. I was pretty sure that I would be relatively "safe" that time, but still just as nervous as I had been before. After the usual drive from Washington to California, exchange and drive back to the house. The walls went up when we once again saw the dungeon gate. This time much to our surprise Grandma Elizabeth was also there. She had come out as a surprise for Thanksgiving.

As soon as papa parked Grandma Elizabeth practically ripped us out of his truck because she was so excited. We hadn't seen her in a few months, which to her was a long time. I can't say the excitement was mutual though, at least for me. Though I tried to act excited, when inside I was utterly terrified. All that I could think about was praying that nothing bad would happen. The last time we saw her she physically abused both of us and took a naked picture of me after I had told her no. The way she greeted us made it seem like nothing had ever happened as though she expected us to trust her again instantly. Haha I don't think so. There was absolutely no trust, but I dared not to open my mouth and just went with it. Aunt Brie was lurking nearby and I knew what could happen if I didn't comply and didn't act excited. Just because she was pregnant didn't mean that she was any less insane.

We did follow tradition and the cousins broke bread for stuffing on the kitchen floor together. Doing that with my sister and everyone else was the highlight of the entire visit. It was strange not doing it in Michigan like we had every year before 2006. It was strange but still amazing. It probably took about an hour or so to prep the stuffing for the next day. In that hour my walls went down far enough to enjoy the task. Despite our differences, we were one family for that moment in time. Thanksgiving day that year had a mix of traditional and new elements. We did meal prep and cooking the same way as we had in previous years. Instead of spending the day inside, that year we pretty much swam and jumped on the trampoline all day. Dinner was more like a small party with probably about 20 people. A stark contrast to the maybe 10-15 in past years. After dinner instead of playing board games we went swimming again and played in the hot tub until long after the sun went down.

On Friday, Saturday and Sunday there was some tension. A few of the family members asked why I was so quiet. They prodded at me and tried to convince me to "loosen up". Most of the time they were also calling me petty names such a little shit head, tattletale and misfit. As they were doing this I usually tried to ignore them. Likely because I was more interested in the book I was reading or artwork I was doing then allowing them to bully me. I do remember Tiffany ripping a book out of my hands and running with it. She wanted to play with me and instead of allowing me to do what I had planned on doing which was finish reading a chapter then play. She took the book and made me chase her around almost the entire house before she eventually reluctantly gave it back to me. Evidentially that made me want to read more so after I got the book back. I found a flashlight, a cozy quiet closet and finished the book. Tiffany went to tell papa something that I couldn't hear. He then came over and opened the door, asked me what I was doing. When I told him, he let me finish my book in peace. Willow eventually found me and also "read" her book until I finished mine.

When we decided to come out it was time to relax. Tiffany under her breath called me 20Q before the rest of the family joined us to watch a movie. In all honesty, my walls were so far up that her snide comment didn't even register with me. All of a sudden it was Monday and we were more than ready to head back home after some rather brief goodbyes. The drive back this time was rather peaceful and relaxing. The gap would be smaller between visits, but I was grateful for only mild bullying during the Thanksgiving visit. Life was good and we were home once again.

Around Christmas I ended up on crutches after I badly sprained and nearly broke my ankle. I did that by falling on some icy stairs. Speaking of icy stairs soon after that happened we got hit with a gnarly ice storm that knocked power out and cancelled school for two weeks. It started off with hurricane force winds and rain that froze over then it snowed. We loved seeing real snow again. It brought back memories of Michigan and sledding. We had a decent sized hill in our backyard to sled on, but no sleds. So we improvised with a massive metal mixing bowl big enough to fit both of us and bin lids. It was like being in heaven. No school, snow and no worries. I even remember forgetting about the looming California visit ahead for Christmas.

When the time did come to go back for Christmas I went from not even thinking about a thing to being utterly terrified. Although the last visit wasn't too bad I did not have any desire whatsoever to go back and made that very clear to my mom. No matter how hard she tried we did still end up having to go back for Christmas break. The drive to California was the same routine of anxious anticipation and the walls going up. This time higher than ever before. What instantly struck me this time when we arrived was the lack of Christmas spirit. In Washington our house was decorated from top to bottom. We had a massive live tree, stockings on the fireplace, wreaths on the doors, a gingerbread house, all the little projects that we made and lights outside. In California the only thing that they had was a tree.

I can't remember if we were in California on Christmas day that year or not to be totally honest. I think we may have been, but if not we did do a Christmas Day celebration. We left cookies and milk out for Santa and the all five of us girls camped out in the living room on air mattresses. We tried to stay up as late as possible to catch Santa but failed miserably and fell asleep around ten. The Christmas celebration that year was pretty small with only a few of their family and friends around. Probably because Aunt Brie was pregnant it seemed more traditional and less like 4th of July.

The next few days before New Year's Eve were much like they had been the year before. Though papa was mostly off work, when he would go to run errands Aunt Brie couldn't resist the urge to do something stupid. She would walk past and smack me in the back of the head as hard as possible and mentally torture me by repeatedly calling me names. For no reason she would remind me that if I told anyone about the past or future "issues" that she would kill my mom. Once even showing me the gun and clicking it into place. Thankfully it was not loaded as far as I knew. Aunt Brie brought it out because Uncle Ben wanted to mess with it. He was supposedly going to shoot things for "target practice." Ava and Tiffany would take turns sometimes calling me "the bratty little tattletale" or a "spoiled rotten brat". Uncle Ben's favorite insult was calling me a stupid little shithead or a fuck up.

    The New Year's Eve party was smaller, but the few people who were there got totally hammered. They were so drunk that they were jumping off of a rock on the grotto of the water slide ten feet up into the deep end of the pool. One-time Uncle Ben forgot to signal that he was doing this and he came about two feet from landing square on my head. Had he landed on my head I would have either been paralyzed or killed in an instant. They were also lighting off fireworks so close to the house that it was shaking. By the way fireworks of that size are indeed illegal in California. The police who were patrolling the neighborhood came by and questioned him about it. Uncle Ben of course denied it and I think got away with only a ticket which I am not sure that he even paid.

    The police did question all of us and of course we were told to deny everything. Threatened with physical harm from Aunt Brie if we told the truth we all complied, sort of. We were inside when they were lighting them off so we had no clue how far away from the house they actually were. We did not deny that they were lighting the fireworks off, but told them that we didn't know or think that they were on the property the entire time. They also asked us if we felt safe staying there, probably because of how drunk everyone was. I wanted nothing more than to say no, I also wanted to leave that instant, but I told them I did feel safe and was fine. Aunt Brie had also said once that if I was ever asked that question I had to say yes. If I didn't she would make sure that Marissa and I were forever separated and she would torture her worse the she did me. If I could give myself any advice on how to handle that now I would tell myself to be honest.

Going back to Washington felt amazing. We were back in our safe place. We fell back into a routine and hoped that we didn't ever have to go back. My mom was planning to go back to Michigan and fight to get papa's visitation rights taken away. Until then she was told to keep us from papa by her lawyer. That ended up getting her put in jail for five hours until the bond was paid. Somehow he weaseled his way through the system and got them back. We were terrified and didn't want to go back but knew that we had too. Papa called that day all excited, I was a combination of angry and terrified. A few weeks later he showed up at my school without us knowing to spend Marissa's birthday in Washington. When I was told about him being at the school by my mom I ran to the door of my classroom, slammed it shut and hid under my desk. My classmates didn't treat me any differently and went on with the lesson. I refused to see him at school. School was my safe place and I wasn't going to let him change that.

Later on I did go to papa's hotel and spend the weekend with him. Just like we used to while we lived in Michigan. It was a fun weekend that ended on a sour note. We went to the arcade and swam at the indoor pool, I think we also may have gone to Seattle. He let us dive off the latter into a relatively shallow pool which lead to Marissa hitting her face on the bottom of the pool and breaking her nose. When he left I was relieved that I could get back into normal life. The transition felt like it did when we would come back from California. Speaking of California, we had another visit coming up that April. We were dreading going, but excited to meet our new baby cousin Sydney who was born that January.

Spring break in California was a crazy hurricane. Some points of it were amazing like meeting the new baby. There were also some incredibly dark times like when Uncle Ben aka Uncle Butthead got so drunk that we had to call the police and stay in a hotel for a few days. Tiffany wasn't around much that break even leaving me alone with the three younger kids when we had to call the cops on her dad. She was around when we went to the desert. Aunt Brie's ways of sneaking abuse were fairly predictable by that point. When I had a rash she would offer to put cream on it, then stick her finger all the way up and make threats. After a while I was still fearful of her, but since I put up so many walls I was almost numb to the emotion. Tiffany was always chipper with the occasional spiteful edge to her. Whenever Aunt Brie or Ava would pick on or mess with her, she would always call me a name or when I just wanted quiet time.

The spring of 2007 is when my quiet side became really apparent. I was much more interested in being creative or teaching someone something then being loud and energetic. I was more of an introvert which was a stark contrast to everyone else. This made most of them see me as a far easier target to pick on, and they often did. What they failed to see was that although I was quiet I loved to build things and or put them together I was fascinated with how things worked and wanted to learn more about everything that was new. My resources were quite limited to learn, but I did the best that I could and used whatever materials that I had access to. I often would find Willow's baby books about animals and memorize the different facts or read through whatever magazine or newspaper had something to learn about in it. They were the way that I could escape.

After spring break we only had one more term left of school before the summer. We went on several field trips and learned lots of new things. One of my favorite field trips that we went on was to the local state park which was walking distance from the school. We went several times that spring, usually when the weather allowed and we didn't have much going on assignment wise. We would spend those days playing on the beach and learning about all of the different sea creatures that we would encounter. Though our little town isn't on the part of Washington that is next to the Pacific Ocean we do have salt water around because we are on the South end of the Puget Sound. Then all of a sudden the school year was over and it was time to pack for California once again.

I didn't even want to go to pack for California let alone go there, so my mom ended up having to pack for me. No matter how much anyone bribed us with the two trips we would be going on, including a cruise I could have cared less. All I wanted to do was spend my summer in Washington because it would likely be our last full year there. My stepdad had been stationed there for nearly four years which is usually the maximum amount of time that he would spend in one place. He was also deploying overseas to a non-war zone location for one year sometime before we left for California.

No matter how little we wanted to go, we had to go anyway. The drive from our door to the meeting location and from the meeting location to "his house" was long. It felt like years went by in the 18 hours that it took to get there. Yet those years flew by way too fast. I wanted nothing to do with being there at all and remember from day one thinking of ways that I could potentially run away. This time no one but Aunt Brie seemed to notice that we had arrived. They acted like we lived there and had always been there. Tiffany even said "Welcome Home" to me. That statement stunned me because I knew that my home was in Washington. My mom had full physical custody of both of us and they only had joint legal in case we were hurt. My immediate reaction to Tiffany's comment was that I didn't live there. I lived in Washington and stood behind it. I think her next comment was "whatever makes you sleep at night". Essentially calling me a liar without saying it directly.

    Both she and Ava went to school year around so they were around sporadically. When they were in school both typically only came over on the weekends but when they weren't in school both were over at the house with us, Tiffany more so than Ava because she lived closer. Summer 2007 is when the abuse hit its climax. It was also the busier of the two summers that we spent in California. So much went on that making sense of it all is something that I am still in the process of doing. Since Aunt Brie wasn't pregnant anymore she could do more which meant that I pretty much lived in a box and was basically numb to the world around me. I could have cared less about anything or anyone. Seeing my face in some of the pictures from that time I see a faked smile hiding a truly emotionless spirit. I was so used to being abused while I was in California that though it hurt I began to just not care anymore. I knew that if I didn't let it get to me in the moment that it would be easier to get through the rest of the summer.

    After a week or two of spending most week days around the house dealing with Aunt Brie's sick abuse and playing babysitter at only nine Papa told us one day to pack a bag because we had to catch a flight to Michigan later that day. We would be spending about a week there at Grandma Elizabeth and Grandpa George's house. This excited me not because I trusted her one bit at the time, because I didn't. Mainly because I knew that I had at least that week free to just be a kid and have fun. No one that I knew of would hurt me or Marissa and I could just let my guard down. By the time we landed in Michigan it was almost bed time for them. Around 7 or 8PM which to us was dinner time coming from the West Coast. I also pretty quickly realized that those walls would still be up somewhat no matter how badly I wanted them to go down. We stayed up pretty late that night because we just couldn't fall asleep.

We slept with papa that night and around 11AM I remember grandma coming in to wake us up. She had let us sleep in because we were now all on West Coast time three hours behind. We spent the next week just being kids. Playing outside, swimming and being with our cousins that lived in Michigan. It felt like the old days. Worry free just enjoying family and friends, some whom we hadn't seen since we moved west. The week flew by in an instant, it was like we blinked and it was over. I was dreading going to the airport and going back to California. I even asked papa if we could book a last minute ticket to Seattle and fly home alone. I wanted to go back to Seattle with Marissa and let him fly back to California alone without us. Despite my best attempts to beg him to not take us back to California, we went back anyway.

No more than a night went by before papa had to go back to work and Aunt Brie would go back to her sick ways of abuse. We also found quite surprise a few days later, a den of rattlesnakes on the far end of the property which was my worst nightmare. During the week going outside was the only way that I could get away from Aunt Brie in any way. Now that the snakes were found we were limited to going on the part of the property that was the back yard of the house because it was surrounded by brick retaining walls. During the week or week and a half that we could only go out to that part of the back yard we were forced to spend most days inside because it's where the pool was and we couldn't be near it without an adult or Tiffany who was 12 or 13.

We were treated like absolute slaves. Aunt Brie made us make her lunch every single day that we were stuck inside. She often came out of her office just to call us or my mom and

Paco names. Her favorites were stupid little shit, waste of fucking space on this earth and smart ass. For my mom she often called her a wh**e and a bitch. Her favorites to use for my stepdad were racial slurs. I don't know how many times she would demand us to come into her office to instruct us to clean the house. Aunt Brie would basically tell us exactly what to do then have each of us come next to her so she could whisper something to us. She told me that if I failed to do what she said or told anyone about this she would beat the living shit out of me until I was broken on the floor. We did as she said just praying that she wasn't serious. She also claimed that Marissa, Willow and Ava were perfect little princesses, so they didn't have to do anything.

Thankfully Tiffany was around most of that week so she didn't have the chance to sexually abuse me. She even saved me from burning my fingers on a hot burner that Ava left on before we were going to clean it. Of course the one day that Tiffany wasn't around Aunt Brie couldn't resist the chance to do something stupid. She knowingly gave me a task that I wasn't physically capable of doing. I think it was something like moving the 50-60-pound trash cans full of dog food from outside or one side of the garage to the other so the snakes didn't get in them and ruin the food. I gave it my best effort, but at only thirty or forty pounds, they weighed more than I did. I just couldn't physically do it.

She told the other kids that I was getting punished for not completing the "easy" task that she had given me. I was ripped of my feet and taken to the usual bedroom for beatings. She threw me on the bed and told me to take my pants and underwear off as she was locking the door. I said no so she backhanded me across the back of the head. Trying not to scream I still said no and she again threw me on the bed and did it herself. First she smacked me across the bare butt and lower back as hard as she could until it felt like I had a sunburn. She then flipped me over and stuck her finger all the way up my vagina and held it there for a few seconds. I wanted to get away but I couldn't. That was one of the only times that I was actually scared. No matter how high the walls that I had up were. I couldn't protect myself from the overwhelming, almost paralyzing fear.

    After that was over she demanded that I put on my pants and sit on the bed so she could have a word with me. I did what I was told and sat on the bed no matter how painful it was. She told me to tell anyone who asked that the redness was a sunburn and that the reason my private parts hurt and were red was because I had a rash. Her threats by that time had become even more extreme. That time she said that if I told anyone she would make it so that I couldn't have kids and would blow my mom's head off right in front of me. After she killed my mom she said that she would separate Marissa and me. Take Marissa and raise her alone while I went to an institution for bad kids. As usual she made me tell her that she was my favorite aunt and how much I loved her before she unlocked the door and set me free.

    Sure enough, papa noticed and I told him it was a sunburn and the redness was a rash. He did ask me if I was telling the truth, thinking it was Uncle Ben who had gotten home before him and had a few beers. I told him that it was a sunburn, the redness in my genitals was a rash and that Uncle Ben did nothing. Which was truth, he didn't do anything, but get slightly drunk. Though getting drunk is bad, it was nothing compared to what Aunt Brie had just done to me. As soon as the snakes been eradicated (including one shot by Uncle Ben) another surprise came. Grandma Elizabeth, Aunt Portia, Kody and Katelynn came in for a week or so to visit. Grandma Elizabeth would be staying longer because we were going on a cruise to Mexico. While they were visiting the already busy house with three adults and four kids staying there, along with the 2 cats, 3 dogs, 2 birds and a horse swelled to eight kids, 5 adults and all of the animals. It felt like a mad house.

To Kody and Katelynn mostly everything was new so they were wide eyed and excited. We had a mostly relaxing visit with everyone. Katelynn did step on a bee that was on the pool deck and get stung in the foot. We all thought it was somewhat funny, but dared not to laugh. There was one time that week when I got a rash and Aunt Brie struck. She went through the same routine of claiming she was going to put cream on it. Then going too far, making threats and setting me free. I often got rashes during our visits with papa because I usually didn't take my zinc or vitamins. If my zinc level got too low, I got a rash. At some point during the week Grandma Elizabeth insisted that we take family pictures with all of the cousins. My first reaction was to say no. I wanted nothing to do with being in a picture with any of them. Though I loved Kody, Katelynn, Marissa, Willow, Sydney and Tiffany I wanted nothing to do with being anywhere near Ava. At all...

Grandma insisted and even bought us all matching outfits that I still to this day remember. All of the girls were wearing dark brown floor length skirts, yellow capped sleeve tee shirts and flip flops. The baby was wearing a yellow onesie and Kody who was the only boy was wearing dark brown shorts, a yellow collared shirt and sandals. We took them in the front yard on or around some rock. When we were all lined up for the picture I of course got stuck somewhere near Ava which was my worst nightmare. Under her breath between pictures she was saying the most hateful things to me. I haven't seen that picture in several years, but I still remember it as clear as day. Everyone else was smiling and truly happy I was smiling only because I had to. It was only partially real because I was grateful to have the Michigan family around, but other than that wanted to run away.

After they left I became the most fearful. The last time only Grandma Elizabeth was there, Marissa got dragged and they punished us by locking us in rooms. Every single day before the cruise we begged papa on our knees to take us to work. We wanted nothing more than to get the heck away from them for as long as possible. He gave in more times than he had in the past and even took Willow with us several of those days. Papa usually took us on days that he had to go to several different job sites so we weren't stuck at the office all day. When we would have to end up being at the office all day he would bring our bikes to work and some toys to make the time go faster. When he didn't or couldn't we were hit and locked in rooms several times for "misbehaving". Much to our dismay Grandma Elizabeth bought into Aunt Brie's lies once again. It was like being put in a cage with lions. You never knew what they were going to do or say, or when they would do or say it.

Most days that we didn't go to work with him Papa would come back from work only to find us locked in a room basically forgotten about. He would usually get so angry that it would end in some sort of fight between him and Aunt Brie. On occasion the other adults ended up joining the chaos if they were either responsible for what happened or enabled it. One time it got so bad that we almost had to call the police. Aunt Brie was so furious about papa trying to protect us that she ripped his shirt, hit him several times and scratched his face to the point of drawing blood. There aren't many days that I remember where there wasn't some sort of fighting between the adults. The fights sometimes made my head spin. They were so wild and the language so profane that it's even hard for me to believe at times. The neighbor even came over a few times if they brought it outside. Sadly, that wasn't too uncommon.

These fights were never small either, they were full blown brawls. Every single time. As time went on they got bigger and bigger and bigger.

All of a sudden the next trip crept up on us. It was a three-day cruise from the Los Angeles area of California to Cabo San Lucas Mexico. All of the California cousins and adults were going with us as well as Grandma Elizabeth and a few other of Uncle Ben's family members. The cruise was amazing. Though one night when Ava and Tiffany who were 12 or 13 at the time were left in charge of us Ava tried to convince us to sneak out of our cabin and go do something. Probably whatever she had planned wasn't the smartest idea. She told us that we would never get caught and that we had to do it or we were boring. Ironically papa was the one who caught her in the act. As did some of the boat security after only she snuck out because we refused. We made lifelong memories swimming and just being a family for once. We even celebrated Grandma Elizabeth's birthday at a nice dinner.

Most of us ended up getting sunburned no matter how much papa tried to protect us from the sun. Marissa, me, Willow and Tiffany got it the worst and it wasn't for his lack of effort. He made us swim with shirts and hats on and reapplied our sunscreen every hour or so religiously. The sun was just too strong and our skin too fair. We wanted to be outside all day and all night. On the boat we swam all day. Practically from sun up to sun down. In Mexico we were outside the entire day with only two people that spoke some Spanish. Uncle Ben knew a few basic phrases that included party and beer. Tiffany spoke decent Spanish because she took it in school. Marissa and I probably understood it the most because Paco spoke Spanish to us sometimes. We understood and spoke enough to get by and help everyone else not get ripped off at the shops. The day in Mexico was surreal, the water was blue, the weather warm and the locals were amazing. Many weren't wealthy, but they were happy.

Almost immediately after we returned from the cruise, Grandma Elizabeth packed up and headed back to Michigan. This meant that our summer was almost over. We had so many amazing memories from the two trips, but were ready to go back home. Papa went back to work as soon as we returned to California and we went back to spending most days around the house. We did have to get a decent amount of our summer work done because we hadn't had time to do it earlier in the summer so some of those long days were broken up doing school work. I loved to learn and still do so I found it fun to do my workbook and read. I tried to figure out most of it on my own and avoid asking for help. If I had to Tiffany or papa if he wasn't at work were my first choices and they were usually able to figure it out and help me. If Tiffany didn't know how to do something or wasn't around Aunt Brie was my choice. Her response was usually snide if she even helped me at all. Sometimes she would just totally ignore me or tell me to just figure it out.

When it was time to pack up and head home I was beyond thrilled. I wanted nothing more than to get the heck out of there. I brought most of my doll collection with me and someone stole a few so I was disappointed that I couldn't take those one's home with me. I missed them for a while then got over it pretty quickly. Once we were finally packed it felt like we had run a marathon. A massive wall of excitement, relief and exhaustion came over of me. On the outside this wall of emotion presented as urgency to leave. I kept frantically asking papa if it was time to go yet. When he finally told me that it was, I was so excited that I jumped in his truck and almost forgot to say goodbye. I quickly ran around and gave everyone a quick hug, eager to get away. When I got to Willow she had tears in her eyes and was begging Marissa and me to please stay longer or take her with us. Though I wanted to take her with us, I knew that we couldn't.

Finally seeing my mom again was amazing. It felt like it had been a century since we had last seen her. We went through the same routine of asking her if we were out of California yet, her calmly reassuring us that we would be soon. When we finally were, telling her little bits and pieces of what happened leaving out all of the details that Aunt Brie told us not to tell her. Then as soon as we arrived back home to our little island we went back to our normal routine. The 2007-2008 school year was my 4th grade year. I was so excited when I found out the teacher I had that year because it was the one that I'd hoped to get. She was also one of my favorites. Slightly on the strict side, but loved what she did and was there for me when I went through some of my hardest times.

My stepdad came home for a few weeks in late September for his mid tour visit. While he was visiting, he had to try to readjust to the routine that we had established without him around. It was difficult at times because he would think something was done one way which ended up being the way we had done it before he left that no longer worked. For example, our bedtime had gone back a half hour and my mom either forgot to tell him or he forgot after she told him that. So for the first few days he would catch himself trying to get us ready a half hour earlier than we had to be ready. When his visit was over, life went on. We were just normal kids loving every moment of life in a small town. We even found out the potential places that we would be moving to once my stepdad returned. We would either be moving to Anchorage Alaska, Langley Virginia or Tucson Arizona.

Before we knew it Thanksgiving of 2007 arrived and it was once again time to go to California for about a week. I was terrified and didn't want to go. When we arrived, everyone seemed happy to see us. The next day I came down with the flu. I ended up with a 104-degree fever, a sore throat and a runny nose. We celebrated Thanksgiving even though I didn't feel well. The next day papa had to go back to work and work on Black Friday. When Aunt Brie was left alone with us she tried to overdose me on fever reducers. She would give me double the recommended dose of one of them then try to force me to take the same amount of another. I took the first one, but refused to take the second because I knew that it was too much. She chased me down the hall into papa's bathroom before I slammed the door in her face to try to make me take it.

I refused. Aunt Brie eventually somehow got the door open and started to spank me repeatedly. She then realized that I had a rash in my genitals and decided to "help" me get rid of it. Instead of helping me get rid of it by properly and respectfully putting cream on it with clean hands, she molested me. I was taken into papa's room because he wasn't home and it was the closest. The door was locked and with dirty hands she put cream on it and stuck her finger up my vagina to the point that it started bleeding. Not only that, but by the time my mom got to me it was a full blown infection that she had caused by doing it with dirty hands. She did the same thing every day minus making it bleed until my mom came to pick my sister and me up. Though I didn't feel well at all I tried to enjoy being around my cousins and papa who was also under the weather slightly.

I didn't say goodbye to anyone but Willow that time and neither did Marissa. As soon as my mom saw me she knew that something was seriously wrong. My fever was sky high so she drove to the nearest military hospital. After I pulled a puss filled wad of toilet paper out of my underwear, the doctors began to suspect sexual abuse. They ran a sexual abuse test on me that came back negative. Not because it didn't happen but because it was a female and she hadn't broken my Heiman. I was still afraid to talk about the sexual abuse and didn't know what to call it or how to describe it so I didn't. Even though the sexual abuse series came back negative I had several other infections in that region from it as well as strep throat and something else that I can't remember the name of. After that little incident the military decided to step in and was ready to terminate papa's visitation rights once and for all.

      Soon after we returned home from Thanksgiving my mom got a call from papa. She ignored the first one thinking that he had to be pulling her leg to get his visitation rights back. When he called again she gave him thirty seconds to say whatever he had to say before she hung up. She was fuming. She also said that unless there was something seriously wrong, he better not be calling. What he said next changed everything. "I have cancer and it's terminal", he found out soon after we left that he had stage four terminal lung cancer. Not pneumonia like he initially thought. My mom decided at that moment to allow us however long he had left to forgive him. She also made the choice to forgive him and allow him to stay with us when he visited. If he was willing to work towards forgiveness, then she was willing to try. At that moment they decided that they would tell Marissa and me about his cancer together in Washington. This meant we would no longer be going to California.

"Strength and growth come only through continuous effort and struggle"-Napoleon Hill

Even before they told us, out of the blue I remember saying to my mom in the car once on the way home from school. I told her that he had cancer. Something was just telling me that he had cancer. I didn't know why, but whatever it was had me convinced. It wasn't some creepy demon voice that told me things. The best way that I can describe how it felt was like being taught that 2+2=4 by a teacher which is a fact. Except this time no one told me or taught me. I just somehow knew and had a sinking feeling along with it, but didn't want to believe any of it. I even knew the place that I thought it was, which was his lungs. When I found out that papa was coming to Washington for a visit. That" I just knew that he had cancer" feeling got stronger as the days of his visit grew closer. I was nervous because I suspected that the two of them might be telling us that, but wasn't 100% sure.

The very day that he arrived on December 22, 2007 was the day they sat us down on the couch together and told us the news. Papa did have lung cancer and his cancer was terminal. This meant that he only had one year or less left to live. Not only was I right about him having cancer. I knew the place he had it and the sinking feeling that came along with that notion must have been that it was terminal. In tears as he was telling us the news, papa asked us if we would forgive him and spend the next year making memories together. At first I was nervous about getting close to him, but excited that we would have some time to make positive memories together. Paco was still overseas with the military, so Grandma Mary was around while he was there for support. It was then that I went from fearful of him being around. To grateful that we would have one more Christmas together guaranteed. One full of joyous memories and positive times, not hatred and abuse.

Christmas of 2007 was my favorite one ever. Not because we got any special gifts that I remember other than maybe bikes. It was a Christmas centered around being together, enjoying that time and loving each other unconditionally. It ended up being our last Christmas together, but it didn't feel like we were closing a chapter. It felt like we were entering a new one as a whole family of five for the first time in a very long time. We spent Christmas break showing papa around the island that we lived on, the neighboring town and Seattle. We went fishing at the pier on the island and got him lost several times around the neighboring town that our school was in. When we went to Seattle we showed him Pike Place Market, the Space Needle and the Seattle Aquarium. He loved all three places and how unique they were. It was then that he fell in love with the Pacific Northwest and agreed with Grandma Mary that it was God's Country. Before he left he even took us to a nice restaurant.

    Seeing him leave after the New Year was difficult because we didn't know how much longer he had. Though we were pretty certain that there would be more visits, it wasn't guaranteed. Just days after papa left we found out that we were moving to Alaska in March. Or so we were told at the time. Marissa and I were thrilled to move to another place and make new friends. I had always wanted to go to Alaska and see what it was like there. Though it was farther away from papa, I was still excited to go there. About a month later in, early February we were told that our orders changed to Virginia, then a few days later back to Alaska. The military promised that they wouldn't change it on us again. Two or three switches of orders later, we were getting antsy. When it was confirmed that we were going to Alaska my mom bought us clothes geared towards colder weather.

    Then two weeks before we were set to leave we got a phone call. It was my stepdad, from overseas. He sounded confused and asked us to guess where we were going. We all said Alaska. His response was totally unexpected. He said that at the last minute our orders had changed and we weren't going to Alaska. We were going to Arizona not only that, but the movers were coming in a week. He would be home and we would be leaving in two weeks and he had a week after that to report for duty in Arizona. My mom's immediate reaction was silence. The kind of what the f**k sort of silence. She had purchased clothes for Alaska which is the polar opposite of Arizona. That same day she called all of our friends parents and did a "garage sale" with all of the Alaska clothes in it. Thankfully she ended up getting enough money to buy all of us an entirely new wardrobe.

    Now the race was on. My mom had to buy us all new summer clothes in March in Washington which is pretty difficult to do. Then prepare the entire house to be packed up and moved. All of this had to be one within a week and she had to do it alone. My stepdad came home only days before we were supposed to move. The movers were already at the house and had been working on packing for a few days. The day that he returned home was the day everything was being loaded in the truck and sent off to Arizona. It was also the beginning of our last week of school in Washington. Telling our friends who knew that we were moving and that it was our last week of school was difficult. I was however excited to make new friends once we arrived in Arizona. At that age the significance of leaving our friends was great, but didn't make as much of an impact as it would have when we were older. We loved Washington and didn't want to leave and at the same time were excited at the same time to go to Arizona and live there for four years. Knowing that after my stepdad retired from the military we would return to Washington made it a bit easier.

    Our last day of school came and went in a flash. We were headed to Arizona and had five to seven days to drive

1,600 miles. For some strange reason I remember thinking that Tucson would look like an old western town. I had never been or flown through there before. Nor had I done any research or seen any movies that were filmed there. The drive was long and we did it over five days I think. With two full days of driving and three spent with family and friends. The first part of the drive was from our home to Central California around Lake Tahoe where my mom's parents lived at the time. The first part of the drive took about 13 hours. We got in late at night and spent the next full day there. We then drove from the Lake Tahoe area to the Orange County area around my sister's actual birthday which took about six to eight hours. We spent her birthday with papa and stayed there to visit him for about two days. To finish off the drive we went from Orange County to Tucson which took slightly over eight hours.

As soon as we drove across the California/Arizona border I remember thinking one thing… Where the heck am I? This place is strange, but the sunsets are amazing. Upon arriving in Arizona we ended up living in a TLF on base for about a month. TLF stands for temporary living facility which is basically a one or two-bedroom apartment at the hotel on base that you live in until you find a house. When we arrived in Arizona we had no plan because until a few weeks prior we thought we were going somewhere else. My parents decided to look for a house off base because the waiting list was too long for a base house. Also because we heard that the schools were better, After a few weeks they found a house about a half hour or so off base in a planned community. Papa came out to visit us for the first time in Arizona in April and stayed for about a week. These monthly visits became routine and were incredibly treasured. Each of them had the potential to be the last, but we hoped that we could at least have one more. We just never knew. All that we could do was pray that there would be another one, but be grateful for the time that we already had.

Every time papa came to visit, he would bring a few of his things to us. He feared that his family would take everything of his and leave us in the dust. Though our relationship with him grew closer, his with his family became somewhat frayed. During one of those visits he made Marissa and I plaster handprints so that we could forever hold his hand. He wrote messages to us on them once they hardened. His hands were somewhat shaky as he was writing them. Though they are legible, when you look at the writing on them you can tell that papa wasn't at full strength when they were written. About six months after he was diagnosed with the stage four Lung Cancer during a routine scan they found cancerous tumors in another place. In his brain... When those were found and the doctor explained how rare they were as well as the symptoms such as fits of anger, numbness confusion and so on and so forth the fits of rage in the past made sense. For over half a decade doctors misdiagnosed papa as a psych case when the underlying issue was actually two brain tumors. Though he did need help psychologically, he needed it more to learn to forgive himself at that point then to overcome a psychological illness.

Seeing papa's appearance change was the hardest part of the entire thing for me. As was living on pins and needles, never knowing when the dreaded phone call would come. Each time that he came to visit, he looked different. Sometimes very different. By the time August came around papa began to lose quite a bit of weight pretty rapidly. In fact, in August he almost died. My mom rushed him to hospital because his lungs filled with fluid and his blood count tanked. Once he got there a doctor who I wish I remembered the name of at the University of Arizona gave him three more months. That doctor performed surgery to drain the fluid out of his lungs and coat them with something that prevented them from filling up. When she said that it would likely give him a few more months she made good on her promise and gave us just over three more months with him. Without her instead of eleven months with him to say goodbye we would have only had eight.

At one point during that year my mom, Marissa and I went to California for a few days. We made the trip so the adults could discuss the plan for if he was ever incapacitated due to his brain tumors. Since he lived with his sister, Aunt Brie and brother in law Uncle Ben who had been abusive to both of us in the past we had to have a plan just in case something were to happen. We were supposed to meet at a park near their house and have a day where all the cousins could be together so the adults could discuss things. The plan ended up failing epically and the day at the park became known throughout the family as "The Park Incident". As soon as we arrived it was instantaneously evident that something was off, even to me and I was only ten. Something didn't add up in the way that Grandma Elizabeth and Aunt Portia in particular were acting. They were acting happy and seemed excited. Those two being excited seemed odd because of why we were even at that very park. My mom, sister and me assumed that either papa or Aunt Brie had told both of those two that his cancer was terminal. We didn't drive all the way from Arizona to visit Grandma Elizabeth, Aunt Brie and Uncle Ben who had abused us for fun.

Upon arriving at the park we were greeted by all of our cousins and ran off to play with them. It was a hot day for California, but didn't feel all that hot to us coming from Arizona. I remember seeing the adults sitting on a picnic blanket over in the grassy area while we were all playing on the play set. Though we couldn't hear them for the most part, we could see them. I noticed both my mom and papa's body language change several times. It went from somewhat relaxed to tense. Then I heard Aunt Brie, Grandma Elizabeth and Aunt Portia agree that we were spoiled brats. My mom later told me that on the blanket after grandma said something like Jim is not dying. My mom recalled swiftly calling Aunt Brie out for not telling her, knowing that papa couldn't do it. From there it began to escalate rather quickly so my mom, Marissa, papa and I made a swift exit. Aunt Portia called me a spoiled brat to my face as we were leaving. It escalated so quickly that in fear of our safety being compromised, my mom rushed straight to the nearest military base. Once we arrived at the hotel on base, papa decided to spend the night with us at the hotel.

  The next day was set to be our last in California before returning to Arizona. We had all planned on spending a calming day at Huntington Beach. It was just supposed to be the four of us to enjoy the ocean for what ended up being the last time. We did our very best to keep the plans a top secret from the rest of papa's family so the day could be perfect. He even drove his car on base and parked it there when he spent the night with us so they couldn't track him down. Sure enough, much to our utter dismay, his family somehow found out where we were and showed up. Papa's first reaction when he spotted them coming towards us was extreme anger and disappointment. This was supposed to be our day together. No interruptions, no chaos, nothing. Just fun in the sun. I wanted nothing more than to run in the other direction. It angered me that they felt entitled to ruin our day on purpose.

  Before they even made it half way over to us papa halted them. He went over and asked them to not come near his "wife" or kids because of what happened the day before. Uncle Ben was completely wasted so drunk that his nose looked like Rudolph the red nose reindeer and his eyes like marbles. This was our day to enjoy together, not theirs to crash. Initially they put up a bit of a fuss claiming something like he was theirs and this was their time as well. That was a fact, but it was our day that we had planned pretty far in advance. They knew to not try to find us. He didn't tell them out plans, but did in fact instruct them to leave us alone prior to that day. Upon returning to where we were sitting, papa profusely apologized for his family's uncalled for actions. My mom reassured papa that it wasn't his fault and we went on enjoying the rest of our day on the beach as a family of four.

Towards the end of the day after asking them repeatedly to leave us alone it became apparent that it would be impossible to keep them away for any longer. We spent about a solid hour with everyone. Grandma Elizabeth wanted to take family pictures with everyone except my mom, including Aunt Brie and Ava. Papa, Marissa and I politely refused immediately. I was not about to take a picture and act happy with Aunt Brie or Ava, especially in such a treasured period of time. In that hour that we spent jumping in the waves with our cousins life was magical. Papa wasn't sick and we were just one happy family. After about an hour the adults (other than my mom and papa) stirred up some drama. That was our signal to get the heck out of dodge without farther incident. We said our goodbyes to them and parted ways. Before we headed back to the hotel for the night we had dinner at our favorite restaurant on the pier, then headed back to Arizona the next morning.

In the fall Marissa and I started playing soccer for a league team that Paco coached. When papa was around my stepdad often allowed him to join in and help coach. If Paco got tied up at work and couldn't make it to practice and papa was around. He would usually take over as the head coach for the day. Both of them had very similar coaching styles. We were given the steps on how to execute a task. Both were always willing to teach, but they expected full effort out of all of us at all times. The team always started the practices with a mile long run around the field to get warmed up. Paco, would typically join us. Papa wanted to, but by that time he was too weak to run that far if at all. When we were doing drills they were highly critical of every move that we made, but fairly critical. Papa and Paco expected us to be solid players and well-rounded individuals. Just because our dads were our coaches didn't mean they cut us any slack. Their coaching skills together paid off, we finished the season undefeated with the league title.

Shortly after the season ended my mom and papa were planning on having one more holiday together before he passed, Thanksgiving. They also planned for us to celebrate Christmas while we were in California. Though she encouraged papa to spend the holiday with his family he refused and said that he wanted to spend his last holiday with us and only us, not his family. Since he lived with his sister (Aunt Brie) we were scrambling to find a place to celebrate it. Thankfully Uncle Ben's mother who we were somewhat close to offered for just my mom, potentially Paco, Marissa, me and Papa to come over to her house. She was willing to risk Uncle Ben's anger so that we could have one last holiday together. Unfortunately he didn't make it long enough to celebrate Thanksgiving. Papa ultimately ended up passing away on the morning of Monday November 24, 2008 at 6:30AM. Three days before Thanksgiving.

November 24, 2008 was the worst day of my life for more reasons than one. Not only did we lose our father to a horrendous disease. We basically lost an entire family along with him when they showed their true colors. It started off with how we found out that he had passed away when Aunt Brie called my mom from his phone and said and I quote "Jim's dead" click. Nothing was explained, no time, nothing. That's all she said. By the way she was told about his passing my mom thought that it could be a joke and called Grandma Elizabeth. She asked Grandma Elizabeth if she knew anything, her response "Jim's not dead". My mom told her to check because it sounded pretty real, but she wasn't entirely sure. There was no return phone call until my mom called her later. She knew that it had to be true and called my stepdad home from work so they could tell us together.

When we were told we burst into tears. We wondered why "God" took our dad, we wanted him back... Now. We wished more than anything that he could be on earth with us. This lasted for a few hours, but by the end of the day we wanted to go outside and play with our friends. Three days later, on Thanksgiving Day of 2008 we found out that Grandma Mary had cancer as well. Hers was likely curable, but the treatment had the potential to cause another type of cancer that is usually terminal. Sometime during the week after he passed my mom and stepdad got a few rather threatening phone calls from Uncle Ben and one of papa's friends Davis. They basically told my parents that we were to show up to the "funeral" in California that they had planned for a set amount of time. Then get the fuck out of California. If we didn't show up or were there longer than we were supposed to be, they had plans to go after my mom. According to their threats she "would be dead before she knew what hit her".

Instead of going to the funeral Paco put us on the waiting list for a base house so we could be safe. On top of planning both of his "funerals" one in Michigan and one in California his family did not probate his death and gave Marissa and I nothing. His mom and one of his sisters took absolutely everything of his except for a few teddy bears that we made him. We were excommunicated the family. In March of 2009 we moved on base and Paco called Grandma Elizabeth to notify her that we moved. Around that time Grandma Mary came out to visit us in Arizona for what ended up being the last time. Her visit reminded me of the time that she lived with us. We fit together like one family that had always been together. Sometime in the spring of 2009 Grandma Mary was told that she was cancer free. Unfortunately, the treatment that cured the first cancer caused a second one to form. The second type of cancer was terminal. Grandma Mary passed away less than nine months after she was diagnosed in August of 2009.

From the time that Grandma Mary passed until we got in contact with papa's family, I was in an incredibly dark frame of mind. I was completely lost. I was on and off anti-depressants that did absolutely nothing but make it all worse. I once again felt like I had done something to make the cancer kill Grandma Mary and papa. Grandma Mary was like a second mother to me. I couldn't comprehend why we had not only lost papa, but her as well. I loved and missed them both so much. That grief put me into a circle of thought that took years to break. All I wanted to talk about was everything that involved California. The good, the bad and the ugly. Basically everything that I could remember. This was a cycle that came up several times over the following few years. I guess if I think about it, doing that was my way of trying to rationalize happened when I was younger. I didn't realize it at the time, but I just wasn't ready to understand everything and wouldn't be until I was much older.

After my dad passed in 5th grade I started to get bullied. In those years it was just mild teasing that got so intense that I felt I had to transfer schools.

Trying to grieve my dad and deal with the bullying felt impossible. Before that year ended I transferred schools, though I loved being closer to my music teacher at the new school. I was once again bullied relentlessly. I was called horrible names such as an outcast, misfit and moron among other things.

It felt like I was living with my aunt all over again. In Washington, school used to be my safe place. Then all of a sudden after my dad passed and the bullying started, I didn't even want to go to class. It took such a toll on me and my anxiety got so bad, that they ended up having to put me in the hospital for a week. The doctors wanted to make sure nothing medical was wrong. My step dad also falsely told them that I was suicidal and put me in a psych ward for a few days until they figured out his bluff. It was a horrible experience that temporarily made my anxiety worse. Once they released me I finished out the year at that school then transferred once again.

    By that point change was my life, there was no such thing as normal. I was a confused, insecure kid who felt that they had no direction in life. I had music and that was about it. I loved my mom, stepdad and sister, but I was truly lost. At the tender age of ten I wasn't able to put much of my past together. That alone made it difficult to move forward as a "normal" kid. I grew up several years ahead of my peers. We had nothing in common. This made them see me as a target. I had no idea what to do so I kept my mouth shut. I only told my parents about the bullying when it got so bad that I was afraid to go to school. Hence the transfer.

"Never thought I'd be doing this. Nothing is impossible unless you don't try." Astronaut Scott Kelly

We went another nine months before we heard another word from papa's side of the family. Around the New Year of 2010 I asked my mom permission to reach out to papa's family. It had been so long and I was terrified, but ready to make the move. She granted me permission to reach out. So I reached out to both Grandma Elizabeth and Aunt Portia. Neither of them answered the first try. So I left them both a voicemail and hoped that I hadn't reached out to a closed door.

About a week later Grandma Elizabeth called me back, I was thrilled. Even though I was still quite angry about the way that she chose to handle his passing I was ready to move on and leave the past behind us. Much to my great relief Aunt Portia was soon to follow and called me back a few days later. The year prior had been absolute hell for both Marissa and me. The amount of grief that followed his passing felt like it was impossible to get through. For parts of 2008 and 2009 I was borderline suicidal, because I didn't know how to move on without papa. Having them back in our lives was a bright light. It was difficult at times, but not nearly as difficult as losing papa. Nothing compared to losing him and nothing ever will so to be dealing with the issues that his family and ours had felt like a cake walk.

After semi regular phone conversations and my stepdad going overseas with the military once again. In May of 2010 Aunt Portia, Grandma Elizabeth and one of our cousins Katelynn, came out to Arizona and surprised us. As a part of their little plot, I talked to them seconds before they surprised us at a local restaurant. Grandma Elizabeth stayed for two weeks. While Aunt Portia and Katelynn were only able to stay for about a week before they had to head home to get back to work and school. The visit seemed much more natural then I would have previously conceived that it would. Had I known prior that they were coming to visit, I may have been slightly fearful. Back then I was excited to see them, but angry that they kept it a secret. When they came out we were just finishing our school year so we had school some of the days as well as music lessons.

Around the age of ten, just before I turned eleven I started taking private violin lessons with a local string group. This meant that by that point I was taking lessons every day and spending up to 20 hours a week in the studio. Seems like quite a bit for an eleven-year-old, but it goes by quick when you are learning. While the family was in town my music instructor gave me permission to take Katelynn with me to a lesson. I was so excited because she rarely allowed anyone other than herself and her students into the studio. Though Katelynn played the flute and most of the theory was practically in a different language. She did have a ton of fun at least I think she did. Part of me wished that I didn't have lessons that week because I wanted to spend more time with the family. I was also grateful that I did because I was able to show them the new me.

We spent most of that week when we didn't have music or school outside enjoying the sun. Including a decent amount of time swimming. The family was enjoying the sun quite a bit, especially after a long, cold winter in Michigan. To us it since the sun was almost always out, it was somewhat old. Seeing how much the family enjoyed it was enough to help us enjoy the sun just a little bit more. By May the average temperatures in southern Arizona are in the high 80s, up into the 90s even sometimes getting to 100 degrees Fahrenheit. As soon as the family arrived, it was pretty evident that they had no clue how brutal the desert heat can get. In Michigan during the summer months the temperature can be about the same, usually maxing out around 100 degrees Fahrenheit. There is one key difference though. In Michigan there is high amounts of humidity which make it feel hotter than it actually is. In Arizona there is very little humidity which can make it feel more intense, but slightly cooler if there is wind. That being said it is extremely easy to get dehydrated. We took water with us everywhere we went, including to the park behind our house. You practically sweat faster than you can replenish your body.

    We also went to a few of the tourist spots in Tucson while the family was around. One time we ended up thinking that we got them really lost, we later found out that we didn't get them lost. We just didn't go far enough down this one road to get there because where we aimed to go was simply out in the middle of the desert. While all three of them were in Arizona they stayed at a hotel near the base. Marissa and I spent the night with them once and Katelynn spent the night at our house once. When only Grandma was left in Arizona, my mom invited her to stay with us on base. Whenever we had guests over, I always let them stay in my room and moved into Marissa's until they went home. She had two twin beds in her room and I had a single full sized bed.

    Going from not even speaking to Grandma Elizabeth for fourteen months, to having her come visit staying at a hotel for a week then stay with us was quite interesting. It was interesting but a highly crucial step for all involved to begin healing together as one instead of apart. When she stayed with us, I saw a light in her eyes that I hadn't seen in many years. Almost a relief that we didn't hate her. Since it was just her and my mom around the house for a week, Marissa and I enjoyed getting to know her again. We were eager to show her all around "our city" and probably didn't stop talking the entire time. I learned to begin to love and forgive again. After all she was the closest blood relative to papa that we knew at the time. Grandma was our connection to him. Our relationship was still frayed and had a long way to go before it would be at its strongest. For a first step it was amazing. We reconnected in an honest way and didn't let the past determine what we should be like in the present. All of a sudden her visit was over and it was time for her to return home. As she was leaving I wanted her to stay and prayed that we would stay in touch. She promised that we would and made good on that promise.

Internally I was still struggling greatly at the time. My inner demons were far from gone. I was still utterly confused as to what my purpose would be. I didn't think I had one, I was lost. I loved my music and at the time saw myself one day going professional. It was my everything and it helped me grow immensely, but it didn't dull the pain that I was feeling inside.

In my 6th grade year at the next new school, it went well for the first few months. Then the bullying became physical. When it got physical it became unsafe for me to go to school. It wasn't only once either. It was multiple times by the same group of people that were never dealt with. Unfortunately, the school that my parents wanted to transfer me to was full until the next school year. So we had to do it in two parts, I would finish out the school year at the school on base and transfer in the beginning of my 7th grade year. At the school on base I felt like I didn't fit in. I couldn't wait to start at my next school after the year was over. At my temporary school, the bullies struck again and physically hurt me. One of my classmates took it upon them self to do a jump kick and hit me in the knee. It ended up knocking my knee cap totally out of place and putting me on crutches for a few weeks to let it heal. Had I not still been growing, the force would have been enough to break it.

My 7th grade year started in July instead of August because instead of going August to May like kids in the rest of the state did. Our new district went from July to May with three two week breaks. The concept of having a shorter summer was new to us, but welcome. 7th grade was an interesting year that ended up changing my life forever. I did get bullied to the point of two death threats in a period of a month or two that weren't dealt with which forced me to finish the last few months of school at home. However, the rough end was no reflection of the year as a whole. I made a huge group of friends whom I am mostly still friends with today. The group of friends that I made that year was so diverse. Our backgrounds were not at all similar and we celebrated those differences instead of looking at them as a negative. We learned to love differences and enjoy the small things that we had in common.

I also met a teacher that forever changed my life. At that point I was a confused little girl. I had ideas of what I wanted to do with my life, still feeling confused about my purpose, with a huge desire to learn. I was weary of trusting teachers, particularly men because of my past trauma. At the previous four schools that I had gone to in Arizona teachers tried to hold me back. Some even called me 20Q which was a nickname that they used to call me in California. I was not previously allowed to reach my full potential. As soon as I anxiously walked into class on the first day of school, I knew something was different. Mr. White nurtured the learning environment and encouraged us to learn as much as possible. We were encouraged to ask questions and work together. We were also encouraged to learn more about all of our classmates. The classroom was always filled with laughter.

By the end of the first week he knew all of our names and a few things about each of us that made us unique. Mr. White always asked me how music was going. Every time he did it made me smile because I knew that he genuinely cared. Early on he noticed my interest in math and science and that I was afraid to pursue both my interest in the arts and sciences. One day either he asked me to come in after school or I asked him if I could come in after school (I can't remember exactly who asked who). We agreed to meet at some point during that week. I initially went in for help on a math worksheet and science project that we were working on. Somehow the conversation drifted into my goals for the future and what I was interested in. I expressed to him that I loved music and the arts and also had a desire to go into flying, but didn't think I could do both. I was afraid to break what I thought was the social norm and be interested in both. Mr. White reassured me that as long as I enjoyed what I was doing, I could do anything I set out to do. If I wanted to pursue flying airplanes and music or the arts if I had a plan, I could accomplish anything.

We loved our new school district, so in 8th grade after a semester of online school. We decided to give public school another try. Everything seemed fine until mid-year when the bullying started again. It quickly escalated from teasing to death threats from the same kid as the previous year. Much like the last time, they were not dealt with or taken remotely seriously. I was too afraid to go to school and fearing my safety I had to finish the year online. I didn't want to spend most of my time doing schoolwork at a computer, but I didn't have a choice. Just before my stepdad could drop papers to retire he was sent overseas to a war zone with the military. He left a few days before Christmas and came home a few days before I turned fourteen. On the day after Christmas 2011 Grandma Elizabeth tried to surprise us again and came out to visit. We ended up figuring out that she was coming out after my mom was acting strange and talking to her more than usual.

After Marissa and I pestered her for a few days and asked her if it was true a few hundred times. My mom finally gave in and told us. We were so beyond excited to see her again. Grandma Elizabeth only came in for six or seven days, but we were able to spend the New Year together. It was fun to just have some girl time and enjoy everyone's company. It was a bit of a transition for her this time because Paco, my stepdad was deployed to a warzone. This meant that he called us at pretty off times and we never really knew when to expect to hear from him. Grandma one time joked that spending New Year on what seemed like the 4th of July was a first. It was almost warm enough to swim so she did have a point. It was around her visit that Paco told us that as soon as he returned he would drop papers to retire. This meant we would be moving back to Washington.

After an extremely long few months of online schooling I was ready to get back in the classroom. In our district you could choose from any of the four main high schools in the district. As long as you lived within the district your proximity to the school didn't matter. The process was somewhat similar to applying for college because of how different each school was. The four main options other than online were: The biggest of the four schools that had the most opportunities for serious athletes. Although known for having solid academics, they were more geared towards athletics. There was the k-12 school that had super small class sizes and very few if any sports teams. There was also the polytechnic high school where you could choose a program such as car mechanics, beauty or science and train in that field. Finally, there was the technology and arts school with the district's theatre, some sports teams and a good arts and a music program. At this school, laptops were used as a substitute for textbooks. They were issued by the school and able to be taken home to do work on. At the end of the four years they could be purchased if you wanted to.

Before my freshman year began, after Paco returned home my anxiety about going back to public school got worse. He decided to record me on his phone when I had a nasty panic attack and play it for a therapist. After he played it he told them that I was suicidal. The therapist forced Paco who seemed thrilled and my mom who was horrified to take me Phoenix. The two of them (Paco and my former therapist) were going to try to get me admitted to a rehab type facility. That was the most terrifying experience of my entire life and it showed. When we got to the place that looked like a prison they took my vitals and my heart rate was through the roof. Paco tried to convince them to keep me regardless later telling me that I needed it kicked out of me, but they couldn't. They called 9-1-1, when I arrived at the Emergency Room the doctors had some interesting news for him. They sternly informed him that I didn't need to be kept in a psych ward. I needed time to grow and learn to deal with my anxiety.

When I returned home I had chosen the technology and arts school and was thrilled that I did. I was also conflicted because I knew that my freshman year would be my first and last year there. On the way to the first open house of my freshman year our family car got hit by a drunk driver that my mom thinks Paco saw coming but isn't sure. I was pretty mildly injured and supposedly slightly fractured my neck and got a decent concussion. Since I was so young and it wasn't a complete bone fracture. Maybe less than a millimeter across, the doctors decided to just let it heal without a brace. My sister got a massive concussion that they called a "head injury". It gave her issues for about a year or so. She still sometimes has short periods of memory loss, but nothing too severe. My mom ended up with a Traumatic Brain Injury that took a few years for her to recover from. She sometimes still forgets things, but is able to live a relatively normal life as a now once again single mom.

After a week or so I returned to school and told no one about what had happened other than my counselors. I was still pretty sore at that point, but nothing that prevented me from doing my normal activities. When people asked what happened, I just told them that I had been sick. At my new school I made friends pretty easily. Everyone accepted me for who I was. As a bonus, the kid who threatened my life three times in middle school got expelled within the first few weeks of school. A few months into the school year, after fall break which would have been October we got my stepdad's official retirement date from the military, April 1, 2013. We had a few months to move after that, but no firm date. After he retired we would be in Arizona for a brief period of time, up to one or two months, then we would be moving home to Washington after over five years.

All of my friends knew that I would only have one-year maximum at our school. I was initially worried about them being afraid to be friends with me because of the shortened amount of time we would have to get to know each other. One day a few of my very best friends reminded me to just treasure the time we had together. From that day forward, I did exactly that. I made friends and treasured every moment. For the first time since 5th grade I felt like school was a completely safe place again. I no longer had to worry about bullies more than my schoolwork. My teachers were all amazing, some of them I didn't get along the best with, but we made it work. The only one that trying to make it work with didn't happen was my history teacher. Thankfully they weren't the only teacher history teacher at our school. All that needed to be done was a simple switch.

Freshman year in a way reminded me of the way that my life has played out over the years. It started off on an incredibly positive note with no bullying for the first time in years then had a hiccup with the drunk driver hitting us. After the car accident life went back to the new normal. In September our school received the first of three cruel blows that it would see that year. One of our history teachers (the one that I switched to mid-year) was diagnosed with lung cancer. Not only that but it was the same kind of cancer that my dad had. When my dad had it, he ended up not surviving. My way of blocking out the emotion of knowing that fact was to avoid talking about it. All of us just went on and enjoyed our year after we found out.

My course load was relatively decent. I took World History, English, Physics (yes Physics as a freshman), Ceramics, Symphony and a semester of both Health and Economics in class. I also took an Algebra 1 course online so I could play cello in symphony for the school. I loved all of my classes and the setup of the school. All four classes had one lunch so I had friends in every class. The seniors wanted respect and were given respect, but we were all just one goofy class. Pep assemblies never disappointed, they were loud and action packed between some of the antics and pranks that the freshman and seniors pulled on each other to the music and dance performances and games. It was like one big, loud organized party. Everyone there accepted you for who you were and we were all simply a big happy family. Before winter break we had a symphony concert that took several days to prepare for. Those of us in symphony, choir and guitars had to skip a few classes and set up the entire theatre for the 100+ performers to take the stage. The concert was a massive success and stands out as one of my favorite memories from freshman year.

Just days before winter break and midterms the school received another cruel blow when one of our star football players got killed in a car accident. We drew his name and jersey number in chalk all over campus as a reminder of the friend and player that he was. Freshman year was my first experience taking midterms. I didn't just have a few I had one in every single class including my electives. People in the older grades were saying that midterms were the worst and to be scared. Once I got the study packets from the teachers that provided them, they seemed daunting. After completing the packets and studying the tests seemed highly doable. The only one that was a bit tricky because it was complicated was Physics. With the right teacher and studying hard enough I passed it with an over an 80%.

In January of 2013 we got our first of a few false leads about moving. We initially were told that we would be moving to Washington in March. When February came along we were told late April. After he retired we were told late May. The school ended up making the final call on that when they wouldn't allow us to take finals early. I was excited to move home, but had to stay grounded and enjoy my last few months in Arizona. I took in every amazing sunset that I could. Treasured the extreme heat for once and tried to make memories with my friends to last a lifetime. I find it funny how sometimes you think that you hate a place until you know that you will have to leave soon. One of my two best friends at the time lived in Washington. Neither of us could wait until I moved back. My other best friend lived in Arizona and didn't want me to move. Up until the last few days of school I thought leaving would be hard but was ready to go back home.

When the last day of school came I realized how unprepared I actually was to say goodbye for now to all of my friends. It hit me like a brick to the face that I actually wasn't ready to leave my friends, but it was time. I barely made it through the day without breaking down. I had to pack up and leave behind everything that I had built for over five years and start again somewhere else. The hardest thing aside from actually leaving was remembering to say goodbye to all of my amazing friends and teachers. I had made so many friends that it was difficult to remember who I had actually said goodbye to. After I took my last final it was lunch time and we were given the choice to go home early or stay. I chose to just get it over with and go home early. I turned in my laptop and gave all of my amazing friends one last hug before it was time to go. As my mom was driving us back to the hotel, tears were streaming down my face. Arizona would soon go from being a reality to a memory.

One more night to go, then we were off. I spent the last night outside enjoying the sunset and talking to both of my best friends. After a late night and early morning it was time to pack up our Ford Explorer with our stuff, including us and the pets in it and hit the road. The first part of the drive was a 21-hour straight drive from Tucson Arizona to the Lake Tahoe area of California. We spent a week with my mom's parents who graciously welcomed us and our three pets into their home. We spent a week in California exploring the area. My favorite adventure of the week was going to Coloma and learning about the California Gold Rush first hand. We were able to pan for gold, explore museums and watch live demonstrations with a blacksmith who made a horse shoe. The weather was cool compared to Arizona and it felt amazing. I was also able to have a quiet moment with my grandfather and play violin while he played piano along. It was slightly intimidating playing alongside him, but equally amazing to learn from him.

After an amazing week or rest and relaxation in California it was time to conquer the final part of the drive a 14-hour stretch from Central California, through Oregon to Western Washington. Our new home was in the town across the bridge from the island we lived on previously. While being in a town of less than 10,000 people once again initially felt isolated and slow I quickly became used to the slower pace of life near the water and realized why I missed this place so much. We arrived in Washington on June 2, 2013 only two days before my 15th birthday. I was so excited to finally be home that I didn't even care about my birthday. Marissa called the timing karma and thought it was funny because it was now "my turn" to move on my birthday. Though we had been packed and moved for a few weeks at the time, our furniture took a bit more than a week to arrive.

We lived on air mattresses for a few days which wasn't an issue. When our stuff finally arrived we were thrilled and ready to start our new life. I was even able to reunite with my then best friend only a few days after we arrived. It was somewhat awkward, but exciting. In July my mom started training me at the local gym for the sport that I had hoped to participate in later in the fall, swimming. She had been a swimmer in high school and offered to train me. I knew a decent amount about swimming from watching the Olympics and videos online. However, very little about the high school team I would be joining in the fall. The only things that I did know were a few people on the team, the head coach's first name and the team mascot. I worked under my mom's tutelage for a few weeks until a few of the coaches for the YMCA's team noticed me. They asked my mom if I was interested in swimming on the team and if she would let them work with me. My mom happily agreed and I joined the team.

Not only did those two work me hard at practice they would come in on their off days and work with me to strengthen my swimming. After my first meet in which I swam a horrible time in the 100-yard breaststroke race (2:08.80). Instead of running from the sport, I decided that I wanted to improve. I also found out around that time that my best friend swam for the same team. We were as close as could be until one day at practice she decided to nearly end my career. She jumped off the side of the pool and landed on my shoulder on purpose. I guess the cycle of bullying hadn't yet been broken. I finished the kick set not thinking anything of it until after when it wouldn't stop hurting. It turned out that my shoulder had been separated and wouldn't stay in. I only had a few weeks before my first high school season, so testing on it had to be done quickly.

When I went to the orthopedic doctor they decided to do an MRI on it to see what had happened and make sure nothing was too damaged. There was a catch, it was scheduled for after the season started. This meant that I would either have to start the season having no clue exactly what was wrong with it or wait until I got the results and miss the entire season. I decided to risk it and swim, only because what my doctor thought was wrong with it would benefit from exercise. Sure enough it was exactly what he thought it was. It was a condition called multi-directional instability that basically made it easier for my shoulders to pop out of place. I worked with a sports physical therapist all season and was even able to swim a personal best time. I went from a 2:08.80 to a 1:38.50 in my 100-yard breaststroke. A thirty second drop in one season.

Throughout the season though I enjoyed it, I was bullied by both my classmates and some of my teammates. Before I even started at my new school my stepdad told me that he bet I wouldn't make it to senior year that I would give up or drop out before then. When school started something changed with Paco. He either dropped a façade that was up for several years or just became a different person entirely. He became controlling and abusive and fixated on the idea of us moving back to the Midwest. He treated my mom horribly, like she was worth nothing and could do nothing for herself. When Paco did finally get a job, he chose to work in Seattle which is over an hour away at a part time job with strange hours and hourly pay. Instead of get a government job in the neighboring town with steady pay, guaranteed hours and a decent amount of vacation time. He was almost never home and when he was, it seemed like all he wanted to do was control every move we made.

As soon as school started it was immediately evident that I was inadequately placed in classes that were way too easy. Almost everyone with the exception of a few the people that I knew when we were little and a few new friends picked on me. I was threatened multiple times, thrown into lockers and called horrible names. I was once again terrified to go to school. School was no longer safe. My grades slipped and nothing added up. I wasn't picking fights or antagonizing anyone. I just went to school to learn and go to practice after. To avoid getting messed with, I ate lunch in the library alone almost every day. Sadly, it wasn't a permanent fix and the relentless bullying continued. It eventually reached a point when I had enough. I was done. I didn't want to go to school, just to be picked on. At the time, I thought that my only two options were to drop out or become homeschooled. I didn't care which I chose I just wanted to get the heck out of there and live my own life.

My parents told me that dropping out wasn't an option so they would homeschool me. Paco claimed that he would be my teacher, but that didn't last long. After a few months he started constantly picking fights with me and abandoned my school work entirely. On a nearly daily basis he found something that was inadequate about one of us. Just about anything could set him off. At one point I was sitting on the couch doing my schoolwork and got yelled at by him for it. Paco came over to me, kicked the reclining part of the couch in, called me a lazy ass and threw my book across the room. I did nothing but ask him if I could finish a math problem before I took the trash out. Over the next eight months this cycle of him picking fights repeated itself over and over and over. He was never home once again and didn't seem to care at all. In March I decided that since my shoulders wouldn't allow me to play water polo. I would be a team manager. Paco called me being a manager a waste of time and didn't show up to a single game that season.

It became increasingly evident that something wasn't entirely adding up with him. Shortly before my sweet 16 when his mom got sick, Paco left for over four weeks, flew in for a few days around and on my birthday. Then flew out and we didn't see him for two months. By the time he returned home I was already training for my next high school swim season. For some reason he didn't like that so it set him off. He refused to wake up and take me to practice. Paco returned home and went right back to work at his part time job in Seattle. We rarely saw him, when we would ask him to take a day off he refused saying that he would try and never actually do it or just straight up ignore our request.

At the very last regular season meet of my junior year I made the time I had hoped to make all year. A league time which for my event was below a 1:28.00, I made a 1:27.75 one girl beat me by .15 seconds. So I was an exhibition swimmer instead of a counted one. It ended up being a blessing because although I had done everything I could to strengthen my unstable shoulder. My coach didn't follow the trainer's advice and instead of gradually increasing my training to that level. He did it rapidly which caused my shoulder to spasm and pop out as soon as I went off the block. I was disappointed, but the team won the league title and I had dropped more than 40 seconds from my original time. There was also water polo season to look forward to.

Shortly after swim season was over, my mom, Marissa and me decided to take a trip to the Midwest over Thanksgiving week. This would be our first trip back in over a half a decade. At the time I was planning on not going to Grandma's house whatsoever, but as the days drew closer I decided to forgive and forget. We invited Paco to go with us, he said that he couldn't because he had to work. He then expressed that it was because he needed to watch our dog. The plan before going to Michigan was to surprise Grandma Elizabeth. We were initially planning on telling her the wrong date and just showing up at her house. That plan ended up failing epically because a family member ended up experiencing some pretty severe health issues before we came out. Instead of scrapping the plan entirely we decided to make lemonade out of lemons and tell her the day before. Her response was what I had hoped it would be. At first she thought I was joking, but said that she was ready whenever. I think it actually sank in the next morning I sent her a picture from the airport.

    We landed in Michigan relatively late in the evening around dinner time. By the time we got our rental car and began to head over to our hotel we were tired and hungry. My mom grew up there, but everything had changed so we had not a clue what we would be doing for dinner. Of all people Grandma Elizabeth called and invited us over to her house for dinner. I was relatively nervous, but reminded myself to put that aside and accept the offer. So we went over and arrived at her house when she was still out getting pizza. As soon as she returned home a few moments later something beautiful happened. Grandma Elizabeth and Grandpa George welcomed all three of us into their home and gave us all bear hugs. As if nothing had ever happened and no time had gone by. It almost felt too good to be true and just right at the same time. Our frayed family was once again complete. It was a different definition of complete, but it was complete.

"Never give up on something that you can't go a day without thinking about." -Sir Winston Churchill

The day after we arrived in Michigan was papa's six-year death anniversary. I was apprehensive about being together on that day because it was something that we had never done. I opted out of going to church with her in the morning and we all ended up meeting for dinner at one of papa's favorite restaurants. Spending November 24, 2014 together gave me closure. After dinner we went back to Grandma's house played card games together like we used to. It was just the three of us and the grandparents almost making up for lost time. There was a mutual love for each other, not a hint of friction in the air. Just a simply beautiful day. Also very symbolic of new beginnings.

On the day before Thanksgiving Kody and Katelynn came over with Aunt Portia and Uncle Rodger. The cousins broke the bread for stuffing like we did when we were little. This time instead of into a bowl while sitting on the floor and stopping at that. The four of us teamed up and made it from start to finish. My mom and Aunt Portia peeled apples while Grandma was just able to relax and enjoy seeing all of us together. She tried to help, but we convinced her to step back for once and enjoy. Kody was more assertive about that than almost anyone else. It was actually pretty funny. On Thanksgiving day Uncle Rodger wasn't feeling very well so Aunt Portia, Kody and Katelynn decided to stay home with him.

For dinner it just ended up being the five of us together on a holiday for the first time ever. It was simply beautiful. I felt at peace with my family for the first time in a very long time. On that nine day trip we saw Grandma Elizabeth every single day. It ended up becoming routine that I wished could continue. The day before we left we invited Grandma Elizabeth over to our hotel to have dinner with us. She brought over Thanksgiving leftovers and another little surprise... Papa's ashes. We waited six years praying for that very day to come. When it finally did it was more amazing then I could have imagined it would be. Grandma seemed at peace with her decision which made it even more magical. It is pretty amazing to be able to say that on the last day of such an amazing visit we received such an amazing gift that I am still grateful for to this day.

On the trip home it was decided that I would carry papa with me in my backpack. He was heavy, but no matter how heavy he was I was grateful to have the opportunity to do it. We ended up in some ways paying tribute to our life's journey up until that day. We went from Michigan to our layover spot which was Phoenix Arizona. Then from Phoenix Arizona back to Seattle Washington. It fell together perfectly, almost like he planned the trip for us. Papa loved both Arizona and Washington. It was an amazing way to end to an amazing trip filled with so much growth.

In on January 11, 2015 my stepdad picked a fight with my mom that got so bad we almost called the police. Paco went insane and eventually told me to kill myself. That was the last straw. My mom told him to get the f**k out and he never came back. Instead he decided to leave Washington and move to the Midwest without even telling his work. Despite our pleas, Paco refused to come back. His claim was that my mom hit him and he had to leave. She in fact moved him out of the way to stop him from approaching us. When she tried to push him out of the way her hand made a pop because it was relaxed. We had to put a temporary restraining order on him to keep ourselves safe. Following the implementation of the restraining order Paco filed for divorce. When the restraining order was lifted he stopped it claiming that he wanted to work things out with us and our mom.

As soon as my stepdad was kicked out, I began to truly grieve papa's passing. In the years following his passing I always had Paco there as not quite a replacement but close. When he was gone not having any father alive really hit me hard. I missed papa every day and the grieving process once again began to consume me. I was lost and thought that if two dads left me I most certainly had no purpose. After a few weeks of allowing myself to feel that way, I decided to own it. I wanted to be an example for kids who have lost a parent. Like the abuse, the loss of papa didn't define me, it was simply a part of me. I could either grow from it and move on, or keep having panic attacks and go nowhere. It was up to me to make a choice. I decided to own it and move on. I realized that nothing was impossible.

In March of 2015, Marissa decided that she was going to join the school water polo team. She was in the pool as a player and I was on the deck as a manager for what ended up being my last season. Almost the entire season everyone but a few girls and one of the coaches treated me like absolute garbage. Most of the girls on the team didn't care if I was there or not and even told me that. Yet, when I was sick or on the off chance that I missed a practice or game. (I missed maybe two the entire season) they would ask where I was and pretend to care. One of the captains told me that I had to sit in a certain spot on the bus because I wasn't part of the team. I wanted to tell her off, but I knew that if I did she would tell the coach that I was in the wrong and I would be kicked off the team. Some of the girls called me a bitch or an idiot pretty regularly. Instead of asking for caps they would demand caps. Instead of nicely putting them back some of them would throw their caps at me. The team did well that season, but I was pretty sure I was done with them after being treated so poorly.

Around the time I turned 17 I realized that I had been sexually abused. It was the hardest realization that I have ever come to. When I was younger I always had one fear that never made sense to me. I was afraid of tampons for the longest time. It never ever made sense until I started reading about sexual abuse. When I finally realized that I had been sexually abused, I immediately came out to my mom. I was terrified at what she would think, but later on she admitted to noticing me acting strange for a few weeks. My way of dealing with that realization wasn't exactly healthy. After I realized it I felt totally worthless. I hit rock bottom once again. I didn't know how to handle it. I had been through quite a bit growing up, but nothing like this.

I ended up finally admitting that I could no longer deal with these inner demons alone. I needed help, but it had to be the right person to help me before I would take it. Soon after I began to seek help my stepdad decided to come out for a visit. I was pretty angry to say the least. I wanted nothing to do with him at that point, but learned to be okay with it if the counselors were around. The first time he came out I refused to talk to him much. He tried to apologize for what he had done which I was grateful for. I was grateful, but wondered how sincere it actually was. To me it seemed slightly off for some reason so I still kept him at a distance. What likely raised that red flag a little was when I saw a bit of his controlling side come out at certain points throughout the visit.

Over the summer I poured my heart into training for swim season. I trained up to six hours every day, up to six days a week. When the season came it was decided with the help of the trainer that I would only swim the 100-yard breaststroke as an individual event to preserve my shoulder. Though it was in near perfect shape the risk was still there for it to pop out at just about any time. That is if I wasn't trained and raced properly. Of course the coach decided to take it into his own hands and not listen. He "highly encouraged" me to swim the 50-yard freestyle and "treat it like a warm up". I listened to him for a while until my shoulders popped out almost every time. When I got annoyed with not being able to race my race because of that I went to the trainer. The trainer set my coach straight real fast.

By that time, we only had a few meets left and I still had time to qualify. At my peak I was making state times, but since I wasn't being pushed hard enough I came pretty close to making a league time but missed it by a few seconds. I was quite angry and after more bullying from some of the girls on the team and the assistant coach. I had a panic attack at a meet. Once again I didn't make the time and was embarrassed. The other seniors on the team treated me like a three-year-old the entire season. The assistant coach seemed to think I was a nuisance. It wasn't the first time someone had wrongly felt that way about me. The rude comments and remarks still hurt, but I stopped caring after a certain point.

On October 6, 2015 while I was warming up for a race, one of my own teammates ended my high school career. I had just turned on the wall and was doing a pullout off the wall, when I saw feet on the bottom. Those feet were jumping around so I tried to swerve and avoid getting hit. That failed and one of my own teammates did a cannonball onto my back, head and neck. My knees hit the bottom thank God instead of my face, but I still ended up getting pretty messed up. I ended up with a Grade 2 concussion and bone, muscle and ligament damage in my back that wasn't immediately apparent.

The athletic trainer treated the concussion which I had to sit out a week for then let me get back in the water. I swam one final race before my career came to an early end. In that race I made less than a second off of a league time. I was so close, but my body just couldn't go any faster. After that meet when I was practicing turns I noticed that something didn't add up. I couldn't get my knees up high enough to do a legal turn. That was the point when we decided that I could no longer swim. Even though I couldn't swim I was determined to still be a part of the team in any way that I could. I decided to step up and help Marissa out as a second manager. The dynamic between the two of us working together was new and interesting, but we made it work. That time helped us grow closer and learn to work together better.

As the new "manager" the team started to once again treat me like crap. Most of them called me a one hit wonder, a freak, a dropout and a failure among other things. I had to learn to ignore it and move on for the girls that did care. They were worth more to me than a few idiots, so was the integrity of the team as a whole. I wanted that team to succeed and was determined to help make that happen however I could. Paco came out to visit for Thanksgiving which was interesting. It was a pretty positive visit. I even decided to take a risk and go visit him in the Midwest to look at a college. We left on November 28, 2015 which I later found out was the same day that I was baptized into our church. I was in the Midwest for a total of five crazy days including travel days. One of those days was a free day, one was for a college visit and the last full day was going to be spent in Michigan. I was close enough to be able to visit Michigan, drive back and catch a flight the next day.

Shortly before I left for the Midwest my mom introduced me to her author friend Jody who changed my life forever. At the time I had recently began writing poetry again and wanted an unbiased opinion on it. Her opinion surprised me because it was a positive one. Having grown up around different types of abuse and so much uncertainty has given me a tendency to not always believe on myself. Jody told me something that my dad had told me before he passed which was that I had an amazing story to tell. My story was one that would inspire so many others. She even mentioned the name of a publisher. At first I politely declined, but did explain to her that I didn't think I was ready just yet. I needed more time to come to grips with everything that happened in my past before I could put it all on paper. For some reason I felt like waiting would make the process of doing it easier.

When I met her I had previously tried to write a book in a binder. I think what stopped me from pursuing it then and there was realizing that I had a solid idea, but it wasn't refined enough yet. Or so I thought. The mistake that I made with my most recent previous attempt trying to force myself to write it in a certain way I wanted everything to fit into a box that it was never meant to fit in. I wasn't allowing myself any freedom of expression. When I finally decided to give up on the idea of putting it into a box everything changed and I began to draw inspiration, but not yet begin the writing process. I expressed this to both Jody and my mom who consistently reassured me that something would come out of this. One of my greatest inspirations was a song called "Roses and Violets" by Alexander Jean. It was a song that I soon became obsessed with after I heard it on my papa's death anniversary. It told such an amazing story, that at the time I was unable to see.

"We can dwell on challenges. Or create possibilities"-Jody Doty

Once I finally saw the story that it depicted, everything began. I wrote "Loss in a Young Life" on January 9, 2016. A story in the format of an open letter to my Grandmother inspired by "Roses and Violets" by Alexander Jean. As I was writing it I was positive that it was going to be an absolute piece of crap. As soon as I read it over I saw something different. I saw raw beauty, I saw innocence and I saw me in it. I sent it in its roughest form to Jody who said that she saw potential in it. Jody's answer prompted me to edit it more and send her the next cleaned up draft of it. When I did I received a more positive response and she encouraged me to see if it would go anywhere else. At that point I decided to reach out and ask a few of my mom's friends to read it to make sure that it was good enough. All of them agreed to read it and give me an opinion of what they thought. It was unanimously a positive reaction. I was pleasantly surprised and though I was nervous I decided to search for a publisher. The time was now.

I searched for a few weeks. When I was about to give up I remembered that Jody mentioned the name of a publisher friend a few months prior. I didn't remember the name, but I knew that she had mentioned someone. When I asked her the name, she happily gave it to me and told me how to contact her publisher friend. The best way ended up being to do it directly over Facebook. On February 4, 2016 I sent her a message. She got back to me pretty quickly, within about 24 hours and gave me her email. It was the first time any publisher or published author other than Jody had even given me the time of day. I got the semi typical publisher response of an email address and her telling me that she would read my work. No matter how unguaranteed the chance was. It was a chance and one that I knew I had to take. I ran with it and put a few pieces that I had written into a portfolio and sent them to her. "Loss in a Young Life" went from draft to publisher in exactly four weeks. As I hit send I was shaking. I had no clue what I had just gotten into, but was so excited.

    I remember purposely not checking my email the next morning because I was afraid it was going to be a definite no. I was so afraid that I almost had myself convinced. Later on in the day I convinced myself to check my email despite how terrified I was. Much to my utter surprise it was a definite yes not a no. I was so excited. For the first time in a very long time tears of joy came to my eyes. Everyone was so proud of me and for once I allowed myself to celebrate an accomplishment. I had finally done something on my own and could take it on as my own project. The time to be excited was treasured, but before I knew it the day to call my publisher for the first time had arrived. I immediately knew I could trust her and though nothing could be promised. I could promise her that I would work as hard as I possibly could. Before I knew it the work began to pay off.

    The day that we first talked on the phone what I initially imagined would be a short poetry book transformed from just that, to what it is now. My publisher was ready to go when I was, but informed me that if I wanted to write a full book. It needed to be 80-100 pages or more. 80-100 pages almost seemed impossible, but I decided to accept the challenge and take the risk. All of a sudden writing went from a hobby with a purpose to an actual commitment. To be totally honest this entire concept has developed as I have written more and more. I was terrified of the unknown that was ahead. I then remembered to remind myself that the journeys into the unknown often end up in the most amazing destinations.

    The one thing that I had set in stone from the beginning was that I wanted the symbol of this entire book to be papa's handprint. I also wanted the cover to be taken somewhere in Tucson Arizona with the mountains in the background. Jody at one point mentioned that she would be going to Arizona in

March. She was planning on making a stop in Tucson to meet my publisher who is also working with her. I asked Jody when we met up about a month before the trip if she would mind taking me with her to Arizona. Jody hadn't yet purchased airfare and stated that she would be happy to take me along with her to Arizona. I was excited but nervous as could be. The next day we booked airfare. It was official. This was really happening. I was going to Arizona, where I could hopefully take my cover photo.

I was in disbelief, but ready for an adventure. I also couldn't wait to see a few of my old friends along the way. Only a few days before we left, my family ended up encountering an issue in our house, an issue that would force us to leave immediately and eventually move. No matter how chaotic life was at home my mom reminded me that I still had a trip to go on. No matter what I was still going to Arizona. My mom had the situation under control and still does. I had nothing to worry about except being excited. As the trip grew closer I had my doubts about being able to do it on my own. At some point I even considered not going because I didn't believe in myself. The day before I left I finally convinced myself to just go with it even if I was nervous. I am so thrilled that I did. Going on that trip to Arizona forever changed me for the better.

After a late night it was time to head to the airport early in the morning. I was still nervous, but ready to go. I was so nervous that I forgot to eat breakfast. I said farewell to my mom and my stepdad who was visiting drove me to the shuttle to meet Jody. Before I knew it we were at the airport grabbing a quick breakfast before we took off into the gloomy sunrise for the clear skies of sunny Arizona. The flight seemed to go by in a flash with one minor hiccup. I brought papa's plaster handprint with me in my small carryon suitcase, but the plane was too small to have overhead compartments. So Jody took the handprint and carried it under her seat until we landed.

Both of us wore pants on the flight anticipating somewhat cooler temperatures. We were sadly mistaken as far as that went and changed into shorts as soon as we got off the plane. When we arrived in Tucson my best friend who I hadn't seen in three years picked me up from the airport. I was beyond thrilled that we were able to spend that entire day together. Just like old times, we were as close as ever and treasured every moment. I wished I had more time, but was grateful for whatever I had. I realized that on that Sunday I had the privilege of being around true friends. None of us cared about our differences in location or background, how much or little time we had together or how long it had been since we were last together. We just naturally picked up where we left off. I felt welcomed by a group of friends my own age for the first time in years. Something I will always treasure along with all of them as my truest friends.

The next day (Monday) was the other day that I had looked forward too since the entire thing began. I was about to meet my publisher in person in person for the very first time. I was also set to take my cover photos, decide on a title and approximate deadline to be finished by. We initially met in the lobby of our hotel then headed over to lunch outside at a restaurant nearby. I had never been more grateful to see and feel the intense Arizona sun. It's something I often said I hated while we lived there. Truth is I loved the sun, but got to be too much after a while. After we met with the publisher, I was set to take my cover photo. I had a vision in mind but had a few ideas for location. The idea I had was quite specific. We chose Sabino Canyon National Park just outside of Tucson. It was perfect, but hot. I would endure the heat any day for the pictures Jody's friend captured. That entire day felt like a total dream. I didn't want it to end. I was in my second home and only had one more day to treasure being there before we moved on to Phoenix. My nerves were gone and life was amazing. It felt like I was coming home in a way to my second home.

On our final day in Tucson we decided to go to one of the national parks in the area. That is after we made one quick stop at the middle school where the bullying in 7th and 8th grade happened. I wanted to deliver a handwritten thank you latter to Mr. White, my 7th grade math and science teacher. Mr. White changed my life. I wanted to properly thank him for always believing in me and breaking past that wall I had put up. He was also the first teacher since 4th grade that I fully trusted. I tried to write the letter on the plane and got a decent amount done, but it didn't feel right. I ended up finishing it the night before and it was exactly what I hoped it would be. Though he wasn't in that day because it was spring break, the office was open and I was able to deliver it to the school. Just being on the campus was healing. In those few minutes I let go of so much and started a few chapter of my life. I grew.

Before we went to the national park I was able to visit with another close friend who was busy on Sunday when I arrived. We chose to go to Saguaro National Park near where I lived and went to school. I had never actually been there so it was an adventure for all of us. It was amazing, the desert was alive in the vibrant yellows, purples and greens of spring that are so prevalent in the desert. The mountains were clear and the sky bright blue. It seemed symbolic to be there near the end of our time in Tucson. It was somewhere that papa always wanted to see, but never had the chance to. As we explored Saguaro National Park, I remembered something quite amazing. Though papa had never been to that specific park, he had been to Sabino Canyon National Park once. It must have been his sign that I have chosen the right path to take in life. It was then that I realized how truly magical our trip to Arizona was. It was meant to be. Another thing I forgot to mention earlier is that we arrived in Tucson on March 13. Exactly 8 years to the day that my family and I first arrived in Arizona.

In the blink of an eye our time in Tucson was over and we were headed to Phoenix. It dawned on me that I hadn't actually been to Phoenix, (except for an hour at the airport in 2014) since the last time Paco tried to admit me to a psych ward. I remember praying to God that my negative associations with Phoenix wouldn't get the best of me and ruin the trip. That was the only time during the trip where I thought that I might panic. In that moment I reminded myself that this trip was about new beginnings. It was time to heal and move on and Phoenix now had a new meaning to me. A positive one. As we drove through the sprawling urban city in the middle of the desert on the way to Scottsdale. I became excited for what was ahead. Almost four jam packed days filled with two spring training baseball games some free time and travel among other things.

On St. Patrick's Day we went to the first of the two games when Chicago played Arizona at a park in Mesa. It was an early evening game. We had lawn seats in outfield. I have been to several baseball games growing up. None of them even compared to spring training. Everyone at the game was simply a baseball fan. No one cared who won or lost, it was just meant to be a day out with family and friends. Chicago took home the win that night over Arizona 15-4. Though Arizona lost that night I had always wanted to see them play live so it was worth it. On Friday it was time to go to another game. This time a mi-day game in Peoria. Our home team from Seattle was playing Texas. Our seats were behind third base so close to the field that we could hear the clap of the pitch hitting the catcher's glove and the strike of the ball on the bat. It was a hot day but Seattle won 7-1 which in itself made dealing with the heat worth it.

Arizona played out perfectly. It was exactly what I needed to grow and find me. I learned my purpose and saw a future for the first time in a long time. I could begin to heal old wounds and pave new paths through life. I learned to hold myself accountable to a promise that I make. Not only to the people who I make it to, but to myself. I became okay with who I am as a writer. Over that week I found the words to describe me as a writer. Two simple words… Perfectly flawed. Not everything has to go into a box to make sense. Life is an amazing gift that shouldn't be taken for granted. I learned to treasure the small things such as swimming outside every day in the warm sun. Seeing the cacti on the side of the road and mountains in every direction that are as clear as day.

My life isn't perfect. No ones' is and that's okay. After many years of soul searching I found my purpose when I least expected to. My friends have sometimes told me in the past that they have no purpose because they don't know what they want to do with their life. The truth is I was there once as well. What I realized is that you almost always find your purpose when you aren't trying to. Having doubters is a part of life. God knows I have had my fare share. For a while I believed them and let them stop me from succeeding. This book is a perfect example. This is my fourth time trying, but the only one where ignored the doubters. Here I am now, finished with it and ready to fight on. I am ready to take on the world now and not let anything stop me. If you doubted me and didn't think, I would succeed. Here's the proof. I am a success because I never gave up even if it took a few tries. Success isn't defined by what you do; it is defined by if you give up or not. Never give up!

"I had to forgive a person who wasn't even sorry... that's strength."- Twisted Angel

Reflection

Dear Readers and everyone who has supported me along this journey,

I am a teen with on a mission. I am a firm believer that anything can happen to anyone. Everyone will go through trials and tribulations, but you can't let those hard times break you. I experienced many, especially in my younger years. I went through nearly two years of horrible abuse by family members on my dad's side of the family. My mom wanted to stop it but was unaware of the full extent because I was too afraid to tell her the truth. My biological father also turned out to be unaware of most of it (not all of it), but most of it and for a time did anything that he possibly could to keep his visitation rights or get them back. His eureka moment came in the form of a terminal cancer diagnosis at the age of 41.

During papa's last year I learned the definition of forgiveness and the meaning of life. Though papa fixed his wrongs with us that doesn't stand true for the rest of our family. Some other family members and friends still don't know the full truth about Marissa's and my past. They know that the abuse happened or at least I think that they do. However, they are mostly unaware of the full extent of the abuse. Something I promised papa I would do is explain to them the truth about my past when I was ready. Recently I have begun the process of doing that, but it is quite a bit more difficult than I conceived it would be at the age of ten. I made that promise at the tender age of ten and I am determined to follow through with it. No matter how long it takes me to succeed, I will succeed.

During those times that the abuse was ensuing I was either utterly confused or totally numb to my surroundings. Life in California was so chaotic that I almost expected to be hurt. I never knew when it was coming, but I knew that it would come eventually. Being so young enduring that kind of abuse was confusing because of how vastly different my life with my mom and Paco was. Neither of them ever dared to lay a hand on either of us or treat us like Aunt Brie did. We were respected and treated like little princesses with my mom and stepdad. Though we lived a structured life, we were loved and knew that we were loved.

From about the ages of 10-15 or 16 most of what I remembered was the physical and verbal abuse. I allowed this to internally consume me for several years. There were time periods every so often until I was about 16 or 17 when all I could think about was California. All of the positives and negatives all melded together for the longest time. I tried to rationalize everything and make it fit into a box. I thought that those memories were something that I could control. I became obsessive and wanted control over a time period that had no rhyme or rhythm. I craved validation from those who hurt me for the longest time. I often took out my frustration in spirts of anger directed at those around me because they were safe. They would never dare do judge me no matter how volatile I may have been at times.

In 2015 I hit a key milestone when I learned to cope in life without a father in the home or that I could talk to. It was the first time when I would see my friends and their fathers together and occasionally wished that I could have the same thing. That didn't last for long, but acknowledging that it was a normal emotion and allowing myself to feel the pain of hat emotion helped me overcome it. I grew to a point where I was comfortable with having a single mom again. My stepdad Paco is in my life sparingly at the current time. We have a somewhat frayed relationship and rarely talk. When we do talk it's civil and we get along, but I wouldn't really consider him a dad.

I realized that I had been sexually abused at the age of 17 after reading an article that I came across. I also watched a TV documentary related to the topic and quickly put two and two together. My fear of tampons made sense. I had been sexually abused. I went into a bout of depression where the world seemed like it was spinning around me, but I was going absolutely nowhere. I allowed myself to feel that way for a while. At some point my mom forced me to get help. She even went as far as threatening to not allow me to swim my senior year if I didn't. I was angry that she threatened to take swimming away from me and for a while didn't care or think she would do it. When I realized that she was serious I reluctantly gave in and am glad that I did.

About a year before recalling the sexual abuse I picked up an old hobby...writing. I have been writing poetry and journaling since the age of five. When I was little journaling was something my mom had me do to practice my writing skills. It then became something I did in my free time. Eventually it morphed into my first solid attempt at writing a book when I was maybe 8-9. It was going to be called "The Life of a Military Brat" I got maybe two or three pages in and lost interest. I tried writing off of that title a few years later, but once again lost interest. When I was 16-17 I decided to try again focusing on my story as a whole. That attempt didn't work well either, not because I didn't want it or got discouraged the idea of it wasn't unique or solid enough to go farther than 30 pages or so. Likely because I tried to once again fit everything into a certain box.

After I saw that attempt going nowhere I reached out to a friend of my mom's that she had mentioned was a local author. Her name was Jody. We talked for a few months over social media, we then decided to meet in person. Jody encouraged me to work on that attempt at a book more until it just didn't happen. Both her and my mom told me to not give up and keep writing.

Soon after that attempt failed and I wrote more I got in contact with my publisher after I wrote "Loss in a Young Life". The idea of writing "The Newfound Legacy" in such an unconventional style stemmed from how I remembered everything. The first part was designed to put you where I was just before I turned 17 by the time you finished reading it. I knew what had happened, but had no way to connect it. Around January of 2016 everything all of a sudden made sense, hence the clarity in the second part of the book. No kid should suffer from abuse! I realize that since I did I can be the voice for those who feel that they don't have one. You can too. Instead of looking at this as a sob story, you can take my experiences and start the discussion. I forgive my abusers with my full heart, but that doesn't mean that I am not angry at them for what they did. Abuse can happen to anyone, but so can forgiveness. Again thank you all so much for your support in helping this lifelong dream become a reality. I may be only 18, but I am on a mission. This is the first of hopefully many to come.

Until Next Time

-Alana Gorski (A.L. Gorski) Author

The Newfound Legacy

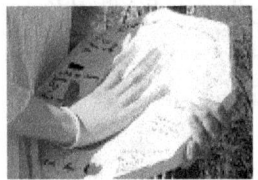

The handprint I am holding in the picture above is the one I mentioned in the book. It adorns both covers and holds the key to my heart. My dad made them for my sister Marissa and I before he passed. That handprint is one of my major inspirations in writing this book because of how much courage it took for papa to want to do something like that for us. The handprint along with a few pictures that I have will be the way that my future husband and kids will know who he was. It is the only way that I can imagine how tall he was. The only way that I can hold his hand or know of anything that he said to me or wanted me to remember. It is one of my most prized possessions and always will be. It is something that I will forever treasure and hold close to my heart. It is my dad's legacy, but also mine to do with as I please. It is *The Newfound Legacy.*

"I have faith that there's a master plan and that even if we don't understand it and it's heartbreaking, there's a reason. And I hold onto that." -Terri Irwin

The following few pages are from an interview that I did with a close family friend earlier this spring for a college leadership paper. Thank you so much Jennifer Eckert for allowing me to include it in my book. It embodies everything that I stand for. Side note: The paper also received a perfect score.

Humility Grace, and Forgiveness: A Memoir of a Young Leader

Jennifer Eckert

Grand Valley State University

Humility, Grace, and Forgiveness: A Memoir of a Young Leader

Leadership defined by a wise seventeen-year-old goes something like this: leadership encompasses passion and determination to achieve a goal (A. Gorski, personal communication, April 5, 2016). This paper will discuss an interview with this young leader as she recounts her past and explains her intent to change the stigma surrounding sexual abuse. This paper will provide history on a piece of Alana's life which has guided her to pursue her current leadership role as she begins to create social change. Discussion about leadership style both as defined by Alana and as the type of leader I see Alana to be will be reviewed throughout the paper. And, as with all leadership roles successes do not come without challenges. These, too will be discussed. I will annotate Alana's suggestions for college students interested in supporting this topic and provide resources Alana recommends to bring awareness to this taboo subject matter. Finally, I will explain the leadership lessons I can apply from this interview into my own life and my approach to, and understanding of leadership.

Alana experienced abuse as a child, sexually between the ages of 7-9 and was verbally bullied and threatened between 7-15 years of age. The vast majority of this abuse came directly from close family members. Ans all of this happened, unknowingly, under her father's care. However, the abuse was suppressed for many years. It was not until this past year that Alana began to recall what happened to her during her childhood. The way Alana chose to deal with these recollections was to write about them in poetry style and share them with others. Alana does not want to see this happen to anyone else; so, she has committed herself to becoming a voice for those too scared to speak, and encourage their voices to be heard.

"New leaders can learn to become effective motivators when they lead and teach by example" (Fallon, 2015). Alana decided to use her gift of writing to speak out about her experiences in hopes to open the door for further conversation about sexual abuse. Her ultimate goal is to put an end to the stigma surrounding the topic of sexual abuse. This is when her idea to use her writing to speak out began to snowball - within three months her idea to publish a book of her abusive experiences turned into poetry became a reality.

> Everything happened within a few months. It all began in September of 2015 when I met my mentor in hopes to maybe one day publish poetry. Then January 9, 2016 came along, that was the day I wrote a piece that would change everything. ...After rereading *Loss in a Young Life* I saw promise in it that I hadn't seen before...three weeks later I decided to muster up the courage and ask my mentor the name of the publisher that she had mentioned a few months earlier. ...I sent [the publisher] a Facebook message doubting that she would even bother to return the message. ...later that day she [responded] ...and said she would read my work but couldn't make any promises. Exactly three weeks to the day I nervously sent her the piece. About 12 hours later I got an email back and it was a definite yes. ...a small poetry book quickly went from just that to a 100+ page memoir. (Gorski, 2016)

Alana's first memoir *The Newfound Legacy* is planned to be released the summer of 2016 on Amazon.com. The figure of her father's handprint in plaster symbolizes humility, grace, and forgiveness. Simply explained, learn to accept what happened, forgive, and move on.

Alana's dream to acknowledge to the world that sexual abuse is not taboo and raise awareness to the reality that this happens everywhere is something of great value and needs to be talked about. These kinds of terrible experiences happen daily; bringing awareness of this issue is the goal Alana has set to achieve. She wants to change the perception on how the public views and reacts to sexual abuse - the discussion of sexual abuse, the emotional damage that is associated with the abuse, the poison it brings to one's soul, and the pain it spreads to those surrounding the victim. Her goal is to change this stigma anyway possible in hopes to stop the abuse quickly.

When asked how she would define her leadership style, Alana responded with two words - passionate and determined. "You can't create passion without feeling emotion behind it first" (A. Gorski, personal communication, April 5, 2016). I would add that Alana is dedicated to her cause in creating change to the way sexual abuse is viewed. Alana further depicts a leader as, "someone who wants to make change or stand out." To couple with this description, Alana suggests to, "get people emotionally invested using personal accounts." All of the aforementioned can be seen in the style of an authentic leader.

An authentic leader can be described as one who encompasses positive psychological capacities combined with moral reasoning, and incorporated with critical life events. This creates a leader whose capacities include: self-awareness and personal insights; an internalized moral perspective to use internal moral standards and values to guide behavior; balanced processing to analyze information objectively and remain unbiased; and relational transparency to be open and honest in presenting her true self to others (Northouse, 2016, pgs. 202-203).

As with any leadership role, however, it does not come without its challenges. An important aspect that leaders must consider is criticism. "As a leader criticism is something you should expect" (Gleeson, 2014). Further suggestion by this Navy SEAL author says to get in front of the criticism; become self-aware as it is a very useful quality as one carries the load of a leadership role.

Alana has experienced this criticism in the beginning stages of this poetry writing and newly found career path. She has been threatened to be sued by family members, criticized on Facebook, and told that she doesn't know what she's getting into. Others are going as far as to tell her that she is missing her teenage years by diving deeply into a subject matter so intensely undiscussed by the public - a taboo topic. They feel as if she is taking her teenage years too seriously.

Further, acknowledging what happened so many years ago came with its own set of emotional challenges. In fact, it came with a plethora of challenges for Alana. Identifying that the abuse took place was difficult. Then trying to figure out what to do about it proved even more difficult. It was through the help of her mentor that aided Alana to push through the confusion and heartache, and ultimately encouraged her to speak out. However, in doing so, she has been, and currently is being scrutinized via social media. "There is no proper way to go about bringing a voice to this," Alana expressed.

It took great courage for Alana to overcome her fear of speaking out. But, overcoming fears is a large part of becoming a successful leader. Alana has taken the first step of overcoming her fear of speaking out with tremendous support from her mother, other family members, friends, her mentor, and publisher. Alana continues to move forward at great speed by way of this support.

When asked what suggestions she would have for college students interested in this topic Alana said, "If you've been abused, don't be afraid to reach out" (personal communication, April 5, 2016). Her goal is to see a domino effect; when one person stands up and speaks out, she hopes it will encourage another person to stand up and speak out, and let the pattern continue until we can talk about sexual abuse as an ordinary topic. Because, if we talk about it and others overhear, they can feel more comfortable discussing it themselves. Alana is beginning this outreach across the country and into countries across the world by way of her memoir.

Alana is becoming the next leading spokesperson to stand up and speak out about sexual abuse with the sole purpose of helping others. "Anyone can do anything. Why not do one post to raise awareness? Acknowledging it happened is the first step to make a change" (A. Gorski, personal communication, April 5, 2016).

Author, activist, speaker, wife, and mother Erin Merryn is an excellent resource suggested by Alana when researching the topic of sexual abuse. Named as one of fifteen women changing the world today by People magazine (Erin Merryn, n.d.), Merryn is the force behind Erin's Law. This law "Provides that the Comprehensive Health Education Program requires age-appropriate sexual abuse and assault awareness and prevention education in grades Pre-kindergarten through 12 along with training school staff on the prevention of sexual abuse" (Erin's Law, n.d.).

At 17 years old, Alana is in the 2% mindset. She is living without limits, exploring new things, chasing her dream, and acting in spite of her fears. I left my interview with Alana Gorski inspired. I was inspired to speak to her about my own sexual abuse as a child; so, I did. This young woman will not let anyone or anything get in her way of achieving her goals. She has overcome many challenges - even those that put her family's lives in jeopardy. Alana is courageous, persistent, determined, dedicated, and passionate. This is a short list of traits of a great leader.

From this interview, I have learned that not only do I need to find my sense of purpose, I need to get out and about to do so. By this I mean I need to get out of my comfort zone. There will be awkward moments, challenges, and moments of discomfort. But, my desire must be greater than my fear.

A powerful summary and quote from Alana Gorski…

The day was so surreal and it solidified everything that I wanted to do and allowed me to fully believe that I had made the correct decision. It may not be the easiest decision to have made because it comes with a litany of sacrifice, however it was the only one that I could have seen myself being happy with making. I will make change because I have learned that what happened to me was a blessing simply because I was the one meant to speak up and make change. (2016)

References

Fallon, N. (2015). 4 big challenges new leaders have to overcome. *Business News Daily*. Retrieved April 9, 2016 from http://www.businessnewsdaily.com/8151-new-leader-challenges.html

Gleeson, B. (2014). Conquering the common fears of leadership. *Forbes*. Retrieved April 6, 2016 from http://www.forbes.com/sites/brentgleeson/2014/05/05/conquering-the-common-fears-of-leadership/#1feffe4576f0

Gorski, A. (April 5, 2016). Personal communication.

Gorski, A. (2016). My journey. Email correspondence.

Northouse, P. (2016). Leadership theory and practice (7th ed). Los Angeles. SAGE Publications, Inc.

A Letter to Papa…

Dear Papa,

    I hope that you are proud of who I have become. My life hasn't always been easy, but I have tried to do my best in every situation or at least almost every situation. I am after all a teenager now a new adult. I can't believe that when you passed I was only ten years old. It often feels like you have been gone for a lifetime. Not because I don't miss you, but because of everything that has happened since that fateful day in 2008. I have grown and changed so much since then. I have matured into a young woman whom I hope you are proud of. I don't wish that you would have survived any longer. I know that you would have suffered greatly if you did. I do wish I could hear it from you if you are indeed proud of me.

    I haven't taken the most conventional path in life. Inspired by both you and mom, I am not afraid to be unique. Grieving your passing wasn't easy, but it was purposeful. I learned to remember what a beautiful life that you lived. Instead of how it tragically ended. I draw inspiration from your willingness to go through treatments that you knew wouldn't impact your outcome. You often expressed to me that you went through them to change the lives of others. It was what made you want to fight longer. It made your life meaningful and allowed you to make your mark on this world. Your courage and strength were your most admirable qualities. As was your willingness to accept when you were wrong. You are forgiven for all of your imperfections by Marissa, mom and I. Your apologies didn't go unheard.

    Thank you so much for apologizing to us on your own terms. It was the most meaningful act that you had ever done for me. You doing that set an example for me on how to be humble about being wrong. I remember you feared that you weren't in our lives enough growing up to set a proper example. I am here now to reassure you that in the eleven months that you fought cancer, you fulfilled setting a lifetime of examples. Time doesn't define how you set an example, effort does. You set an example for us by simply waking up every morning no matter how rotten you felt. Apologizing for your wrongdoings and downfalls taught us how to be humble and forgive. Coaching us in soccer taught us how to accept criticism and build off of it. Encouraging us to follow our dreams, no matter how big or unachievable they seemed taught us to never give up. If we had a plan, there was a chance of success. Showing your appreciation to mom taught us how spouses should treat each other. Showing us love taught us how to love.

What more do we need? You gave us everything we needed in eleven short months. Drive, Encouragement, the ability to Forgive, Love, Life Lessons, a Legacy and Faith. Like I said time doesn't determine quality, effort does. In the short time that you had you gave it 100% effort and it ended up being a total success.

As far as faith goes I will admit that I have slightly faltered. I have shied away from the church because it's just too difficult to go back to something that reminds me of you so much. Since you passed I have gone to mass very few times. So few that I could probably count them on one hand in all honesty. It's not God that I don't believe in, I am just unsure of the church for some odd reason. I know that you wanted me to one day be confirmed into the Catholic church. That is something that I have yet to do and am unsure if I ever will. Not because I have anything against the Catholic Church because I don't. I admire it very much; I just don't know if I will be able to ever do it. I remember and think of you every single day, but not for what religion you practiced. If I do, I know you will be proud of me. If I choose not to, I hope you understand.

This book is truly for you. From start to finish I have kept your message of humility, grace and forgiveness in mind. My goal is to do what you couldn't and work towards ending abuse. Writing this I am almost at a loss for words. I feel like you have been guiding me from wherever you are along the way. I feel as though you are helping me write this amazing book and have been from the start. I miss you so much, but often feel your presence. Without the guidance from everyone, this wouldn't be happening.

Before you passed when I told you that I wanted to one day be a published author. You explained to me that I would know when the right time came. When it came in real life, I almost didn't believe it. I just got a feeling one day that I should go for it. I almost didn't listen; I was the most nervous that I had ever been in my entire life. When I decided to just run with my gut and go for it. Self-doubt nearly consumed me. I then felt accomplished when it became a when instead of an if. Writing a 100+ page book seemed like a huge task at first. Especially on the timeline that I had in mind. I drew inspiration from you knowing that you never made anything easy on yourself. You loved to take risks and try new things. Once I got into the process farther, I realized that anything was possible.

Here I am exactly 4 months and 11 days later with a complete first draft. Ahead of schedule. Thank you so much for being my father. You are a true inspiration. I hope you are proud of me. I love you so much!

With Love

♡ Your Daughter Alana Age18

Acknowledgements

To finish off I want to say thank you to a few amazing people who have been key in the success of this book. I first want to say thank you to the three women who have been with me from start to finish Valerie Gorski Luna, Jody Doty and Kellie Fitzgerald. My mom Valerie Gorski Luna who has been my biggest supporter and harshest critique. Over the past few months she has put up with me spending most of my days writing and doing school work instead of chores. My amazing mentor Jody Doty who has shown me nothing but support along this journey. She is also the one who got me in contact with my publisher and took me to Arizona with her. My amazing publisher Kellie Fitzgerald has been such an incredible encouragement and guide throughout this entire process. She has allowed me to set crazy tight deadlines and believed that I would reach them. Thank you so much to my amazing sister Marisa for allowing me to share part of your story. Also thank you so much Jenniffer Eckert for allowing me to include your leadership paper in my book that received a perfect score.

I also want to say a huge thank you to Richard Kangas, Chris Carney, Scott Kwierant, Robert Mannino, Leslie Larson, Debbie Sexton, Sandi McLane Bullington who all knew papa growing up. As well as Taylor Paulson and Jim Connon. All of these amazing family members and friends contributed to the 50th birthday tribute to papa. Without your help on that and continued support this would fee 100x harder than it already does. Finally thank you to everyone else who has supported me in any way along this journey. Your support means the world to me.

Thank you so much Linda Webb for taking the front and back cover photos and the photo on page 16() at Sabino Canyon National Park in Tucson Arizona.

The Final Sign

I can say that papa is indeed proud of me. I decided to stay up rather late for the final push. I have searched for a sign this entire time that he was indeed proud of me. Tonight the urge to find a sign became stronger. I felt like I knew it was coming. It was 12:38AM this morning when just after I typed the final word a song came on the radio. That song was "Roses and Violets" by Alexander Jean. The very song that inspired "Loss in a Young Life" and ultimately the entire book. I listened to it awe- inspired because of how surreal this entire journey has been. While it was playing I was able to have a clear mind and only focus on the lyrics for the first time since everything began. "Roses and Violets" by Alexander Jean finished playing at 12:42AM. Papa was 42 when he passed. It was my sign that this book is now complete. I am ready to take on this challenge head on.

I began this journey excited but unsure of why I was meant to take this path and not knowing if papa was proud of me. I ended it confident in my choice and certain that papa is indeed proud of the path I have chosen. Though a short experience this morning, it gave me chills and was truly sobering. It will be an experience that I look back on decades from now and bask in how amazing it felt. Since papa is no longer here with us I can't physically give him a gift, but I can begin a new journey. My gift to him this year will be to have finished this book and start another amazing chapter in life. Happy Father's Day Papa! I couldn't be more thrilled to begin to imprint our legacy on this world in a more amazing way on such a symbolic day. Life is love and love is a legacy.

www.ingramcontent.com/pod-product-compliance
Lightning Source LLC
Chambersburg PA
CBHW071912290426
44110CB00013B/1361